MW00441253

"Over the course of 15 years as a youth leader, Weston has learned the dos and don'ts required for success in youth ministry and presents them here to spur young youth leaders toward maturity in ministry. Pastors, buy this book for your youth leaders and discuss it with them weekly. Veteran youth leaders, this book will help you train aspiring leaders. Youth workers of all stripes, discuss this book with a friend and sharpen each other as iron sharpens iron."

—Rev. Andrew Mills
Associate Pastor
Covenant Presbyterian Church, Jackson, Mississippi
Teaching Elder, Evangelical Presbyterian Church (EPC) Next Generation Ministries Council

"The only word I have to describe this book is *finally*. *Finally*, someone wrote what leaders need to know about beginning the youth ministry journey and avoiding its many land mines. What makes this book stand out from others is that it is a youth ministry guide from a typical-sized youth ministry. Most other youth ministry books seem to be written from the perspective of youth leaders with large numbers of students and leaders, as well as seemingly unmatched budgets. This book is different. Weston has crafted this book through his very own path into youth ministry. I have been lucky enough to witness his amazing call to serve his church and student ministry. Through this book, you will find a road map to have a fruitful and healthy student ministry. In the following pages, I believe you will find God's keys to impacting the next generation."

—Mike Howington
Coordinator of Youth and Family Ministries,
United Methodist Church Conference, Mississippi

Student Ministry Field Guide

DEBUNKING THE "BIG KID" LABEL

Weston Blaha

CrossLink Publishing
RAPID CITY, SD

Blaha/CrossLink Publishing
1601 Mt Rushmore Rd. Ste 3288
Rapid City, SD 57701
www.CrossLinkPublishing.com

Ordering Information:
Quantity sales. Special discounts are available on quantity purchases by corporations, associations, and others. For details, contact the "Special Sales Department" at the address above.

Student Ministry Field Guide/Weston Blaha. —1st ed.
ISBN 978-1-63357-388-8

Contents

Acknowledgments

To say that I have been disproportionately blessed by the people in my life would be an understatement. I have no room to complain about the field in which God has placed me to labor. There have been influences in my life that God used to push me when I grew weary, encourage me when depressed, and "bring me back down to earth" when I grew overly-confident. If I were to place every name in these pages, there would be no room for the book. However, there are a few people that I would like to mention who have done far more than their fair share of work.

To my father, Jim Blaha. I have learned more about godly ministry, patience, and integrity from you than anywhere else. Father, thank you for being a continual model of the faithful servant who is satisfied and content to serve in every situation in which God has called you. To my mother, Vicky Blaha. You have always been my biggest supporter and encourager. Thank you for being an example of a godly wife and co-laborer in the ministry.

To my good friend Mike Howington, who believed in my calling to ministry when no one else would give me a chance. Thank you for mentoring and opening my eyes to the full scope of youth ministry.

To James Pullen, Mark Stucky, and Greg Molen. You men have always been willing to fight for me and also to correct me when I have been wrong. I have greatly coveted your friendship over the years. Lakeside is blessed to have you.

To Bill Moss, who opened my eyes to the importance of punctuality and attention to detail.

To Brandon Bates, Tyson Taylor, and Philip Anthony. You men have all had an incredible impact on my life, and I would not be who I am today without your help.

To Lakeside Presbyterian Church, EPC. Thank you for your grace as I failed, grew, learned, and continue to learn. You are a blessing to your community and to the world.

To my wife, Candace, who has gracefully endured every crazy idea and undertaking that I could dream up. Thank you for being willing to follow the calling God has placed on my life. Thank you for being this man's greatest treasure. You are a gift from the Lord, and I am blessed to do life with you.

Introduction

"Why another book on youth ministry?" you may ask. As an enthusiastic reader and a fan of concrete ideas and concepts, I have seen a shortage of practical information organized specifically toward one's first year of youth ministry. There are copious books addressing strategy and vision, and even more on relationships and discipleship. As I write, the most prominent current trends are "engaging parents" and the "mobilization" of the next generation.

This is a guide primarily about the first year of youth ministry at a new church, but I believe student ministry "vets" will also find it helpful. Of course, these other books are necessary, but implementing and seeing your ministry vision flourish is mainly dependent on the habits you create while serving in your first year at a church. It is during this time you put in hard work, hoping to see the fruit of that labor years down the road. However, other things could also be happening. During your first year, your church either comes to trust your vision or doubt it. It is often in this first year that you gain the confidence of your church leaders or raise concerns regarding your ministry. Within the first year, those leaders might begin to question whether or not your salary seems justified. The first year matters.

Because churches are called good to be stewards of their resources, wisdom in financial decisions is of the utmost importance. This often influences salary arrangements regarding the youth ministry. One cause for this is that youth directors have burned churches by accepting the position because it was a "fun" job and not because it was a calling. As a result, the quality of ministry and depth of spiritual leadership was lacking. A second reason is that churches frequently see youth ministry as a step toward being in "higher ministry" and not as a vocation in its own right. As such, the position often pays as if it is a stepping-stone. Third, youth ministry is often under-appreciated because many youth ministers have earned the "big kid" label. As such, many churches only expect the "playing" aspect of their youth ministry and compensate accordingly. Due to these and other matters, churches can undervalue youth ministry when considering compensation. The solution is to communicate to the church the spiritual benefits that proceed from fruitful ministry.

At the publishing of this book, I will have worked in student ministry for over fifteen years. My story has not been a traditional one. When I first sensed God calling me to student ministry, I submitted an application to my home church, which they kindly declined. This church was one in which I had grown up and spent two summers as a youth intern. I understood the culture, the parents, and the students loved me. I could not envision a scenario in which they would choose another candidate. Notwithstanding all of that, I was crushed when the church decided to hire another applicant.

This rejection began a journey in which the Lord did much to sanctify and develop me as a leader. Like a rod of metal aspiring to be a sword, I needed to be shaped and molded to be serviceable. This required much heat, hammering, and cooling. Eventually, I was hired—almost accidentally—as a part-time assistant youth director in a neighboring city. After six months as a part-time staff, I received a promotion and became the full-time assistant youth director. Within eighteen months at that church, I had received a significant raise, was overseeing two separate ministries, and completing my undergraduate degree in Social Services.

In 2012, I received a call from my home church—-the same one who had decided not to hire me a few years earlier. After much prayer and consideration, I accepted the position. I have now been serving at this church for nine years and hope to continue for many more.

My student ministry journey has pushed me to grow. I have served in two different denominations, worked under diverse leadership styles, and waited patiently (and sometimes impatiently) for the Lord to open the right doors. Hindsight is 20/20, as the saying goes, and I can now look back and see how the Lord planted seeds in my life that required the right soil, water, and time to mature and yield fruit. When my home church declined my first application fifteen years ago, it was the Lord closing the door so that I could have this desperately needed time to grow.

One of the benefits of my youth ministry journey is working with diverse churches and leaders over the years. If someone were to inquire about the most fruitful youth ministries that I have ever witnessed, I would not necessarily identify those ministries with the most dynamic speakers. They may not have had leaders who were gifted with the most transcendent charisma. Additionally, the most educated and knowledgeable youth directors may not have been leading these students. Instead, the most fruitful youth ministries have men and women leading with a passion and energy that furiously loves their church. Additionally, this same love, care, and concern was also directed toward the small details of ministry that often go overlooked. Part of loving your church is instilling the healthy habits that lead to a successful ministry.

This book's contents emerge from countless conversations with youth ministers, much reading, education, and training, as well as numerous experiences of both failure and success. If you are past your first year at a church, I believe this book is still for you. Playing catch-up is never easy, but it can be played well! I advise that you approach this book with openness, self-honesty, and a teachable heart.

If youth directors refuse to be disciplined in the areas discussed in this book, it will become challenging to cultivate ministries that please God and benefit young people. Why is that? Because youth ministry is deeply relational. The "first-year" habits examined in this book, if disregarded, will become seeds of discontent. Over time, this will sour even the best working relationships, forming a considerable barrier between the ministry you have and the ministry you desire.

This guide examines disciplines that I believe contribute to debunking the ministry-stunting "big kid" label. For some of you, portions of this book will feel like common-sense information. For others, this book will challenge your entire philosophy of youth ministry. However, each of us must always be willing to learn and grow.

There is a great need for men and women who love the Lord and the church. There is also a great need for these servants to know that they are indeed ministers of the Word. Teenagers need godly men and women to exhibit holy living and faithful Christian leadership. Thank you for your ministry and heart to serve the Kingdom of God!

PART 1

Disciplines that Debunk the "Big Kid" Label

Many talented youth directors see their ministry visions unrealized due to poor discipline. These detrimental habits are unknowingly cultivated during their first year at their new church. As the saying goes, "You only have one opportunity to make a good first impression." For those of us in ministry, this is a precious warning. Those who nurture toxic habits unknowingly sabotage fruitful ministry down the road.

In the ministry field, you are often appreciated because you pour into the lives of students and parents. You are valued because they can trust you to act responsibly and give their children wise advice in seasons of difficulty. You are loved because of the type of relationships you hold with the church. However, toxic habits have the unique ability to poison and de-value all of that. The result is earning the label of "big kid." The following chapters will center on the habits that are necessary to debunk the "big kid" label and prepare you for a long and fruitful ministry.

CHAPTER 1

Debunk the "Big Kid" Label

"The mark of the immature man is that he wants to die nobly for a cause, while the mark of the mature man is that he wants to live humbly for one."
- Wilhelm Stekel -

Inevitably, many youth directors will face the label "big kid." This is not always a bad thing. Most churches choose youth directors who can relate and connect well with teenagers. "Playing" is part of this. Congregations seldom want someone who merely teaches. They want a youth director who can live life well with their students and their parents. This means that youth directors are expected to strike that delicate balance between child and adult. The phrase I have developed to describe this is, "Play like a kid, act like an adult, and know when each is required." Problems appear when youth directors confuse this formula.

Where are those areas in which youth directors sometimes earn themselves the description of "big kid?" Below is a list of prevalent label "triggers" and some best practices in avoiding this label.

Don't be on time, be early.

Do you know who is almost always late? A teenager. Do you know who is almost always on time? A business professional. In the youth ministry world, we have difficulty disproving the "big kid" label, so we must do more than be on time: we need to be early. Punctuality conveys to whomever you are meeting that:

- You value their time.
- You planned ahead to make the meeting happen.
- You can use a calendar for scheduling.
- You are responsible.

If you want to earn the label of "big kid" early in your ministry, practice poor discipline by being regularly tardy or, worse, forgetting about the calendared meeting altogether!

Clean up your social media.

One of the earliest impressions you will make on your new church will be through social media. Some congregants will have determined who you are well before you have an opportunity to prove otherwise. If your social media accounts are full of frat humor, sassy girlfriend posts, or political statements, you may earn an undesired label. Your social media accounts need to be windows into your life that parents would like their children to see. They should also be filled with content that displays an elevated maturity level, not a childish one. Some tips for this:

- Delete anything you are "tagged in" that does not come from a wholesome account.
- Log into any social media accounts that you rarely use. Update and clean them up.
- Set up your social media accounts in such a way that you must approve any comments or posts in which you are

tagged. This keeps that wild friend of yours from dragging you into something you are better off not associating with.

Communicate often and clearly with parents.

I am not someone who relishes administrative work, but clear and consistent communication is a must. If you earn the label of a neglectful communicator, parents will be frustrated and lump you into the "big kid" category. Here are tips for clear communication:

- Send (at least) weekly emails to your students' parents.
- Create text groups for parents and youth to remind them of events.
- Maintain current and highly communicative ministry social media accounts.

Manage your finances.

Sometimes, youth ministry activities are not entirely appreciated by the finance committee or finance department. For example, why do you need forty-seven pool noodles for youth ministry this week? It may be unclear why the church pays thousands of dollars each summer for students to go to the beach. They may not appreciate why the church needs an Xbox. Regardless, what will never be acceptable is sloppy communication concerning finances. How you manage finances directly influences how you are labeled. Here is some advice:

- Submit receipts regularly.
- Label and copy every receipt as to its purpose
- Make sure you have the support of the appropriate oversight authority before making large financial decisions.
- If you realize you will go over budget, address it with the leadership before it happens.

- Be knowledgeable about your church's financial situation. Is it a bad time to spend a lot of money, even though you technically have the budget for the expenditure?

Dress like an adult when in the office.
At any given moment, you may decide it is time to renovate the entire youth space! But of course, parishioners (especially senior citizens) will undoubtedly drop by the church office unannounced. For many, the only time they see you outside of Sunday mornings is during these unexpected meetings. If you are dressed like a teenager in a situation where you should be dressed like an adult, you may earn the "big kid" label. With the senior citizen generation more than with any other, this label is difficult to erase. I am not suggesting you wear a suit, but you should dress in more professional attire than gym clothes when it is practical.

Practice modesty.
There is a need to distinguish between dressing like an adult and being modest in our clothing choice. Ministry demands a higher modesty standard than the world might, and we need to appreciate that code. This is why pastors historically have worn robes: the preacher was seeking to deflect any focus on himself so that people would only concentrate on the words preached. Compare this to today's culture of ministers in fashionable designer clothes.

Thus, we should endeavor to remain modest in clothing at all times, even in swimming situations. Be wary of the personal photos that you or others post online. Dress in a manner that does not cause your brother or sister in Christ to stumble.

Be conscious of tattoos/piercings.
Culture is moving toward a much more accepting and welcoming view of tattoos and piercings. But it is important to be aware of the context in which you minister. The odds are many elderly

congregants in your church are uncomfortable with visible tattoos and "non-ear" piercings. Although you may have a valid and biblically sound argument for the freedom of conscience for these things, I would suggest that this is not a "hill to die on." Be respectful, understanding, gracious, and do your best to promote an image that your whole congregation feels suitable for someone in leadership over the youth.

Be smart with your "non-church" life.

This includes everything from vaping and drinking to movie theater and entertainment decisions. Students will use you as an excuse to indulge in less-than-ideal activities if they see you doing the same. If you take advantage of your freedom to foster bad habits, then the church will have an occasion to examine your maturity. Best practices would be to avoid many of these things altogether, but under Christian liberty, I recommend at the very least that you stringently aim to keep these from being public habits. Remember, you are an example!

Do not have tons of unread notifications on your phone.

This may appear petty, but when I sit beside someone who has 937 unread texts, 18 voice mails, and 1,385 unread emails, I begin to hyperventilate. I assume that person is irresponsible and unable or unwilling to communicate on a proficient professional level. Also, do not assume that people notice missed calls. Utilize voice mail on both ends so that you are without excuse.

Return correspondence with an equal level of professional respect.

If you receive an email, email back in an appropriately professional manner. Remove the "Sent from iPhone" tag from your phone settings. As a parent, nothing is worse than feeling as if your important issue was given the minimal attention of a "redlight reply." If you have missed calls, call back in a punctual timeframe. Whatever method used to connect with you should be the method exercised to return correspondence (unless specified otherwise).

Keep your digital footprint minimal.
The world of wireless phones and accessories is a relatively new one, despite our culture having us believe otherwise. Although you may have "grown up with it your entire life," at age 34, I can remember going to high school when only my wealthier classmates could afford smart devices. Digital footprints are relatively new. Thus, if you are constantly checking, texting, or scrolling on your devices in public, you will be seen as no different from the high school students you lead. Many parents believe that their kids are "addicted" to their various screens. You can easily earn the same label. My advice: keep your phone on vibrate, mute notifications on your watch, and absolutely refrain from checking your devices while having a conversation with others. Give those sharing the room with you your full attention and avoid giving text messages and social notifications a higher priority.

Be sparse with political commentary on social media.
Social media is a poor medium for serious discourse. It was created for short interactions, not drawn-out public exchanges. I would recommend not allowing your political opinions, which inevitably will not line up with every member in your church, to be a cause of consternation between you and your flock. If you burn a bridge with someone politically, you have often burned the bridge with them spiritually. Very often, political disagreements between Christians arise from improper applications of a biblical worldview. Be careful not to allow your parishioners to dismiss your ministry because they lack a correct biblical worldview. Rather, use your ministry to develop their perspective.

The dangers of earning the "big kid" label are long-lasting. Your authority and influence may be questioned if it takes root.

From there, your maturity to handle large budgets, trips, and events will regularly be a topic of discussion. More importantly, the parents of the students you are serving may not see you as possessing the necessary spiritual maturity to speak into their children's lives. If that occurs, parents will not see the value of urging their teenagers to attend youth activities.

Once earned, the "big kid" label is hard to shake. Practicing habits that demonstrate maturity is vital to fruitful ministry in the years to come.

Executing Wise Judgment

Churches need to perceive you have wisdom. Because youth directors often earn a label of immaturity, they are given little slack when using poor judgment. Even though you may make what seemed like the right decision at the time by everyone involved, a hindsight judgment by a self-appointed critic can derail the perception of trust and maturity, which you previously enjoyed. Here are some ways to protect yourself against that:

Use the power of "we."
If you have an adult leadership team or youth committee, make sure they are on-board with any large decisions. This allows you to say, "We felt like" rather than, "I decided." A committee is of immense help for a new youth director and helps elude the "poor judgment" label.

Think like your most worried parent.
I do not believe that your most anxious parent should be your standard for decision-making. However, if you have asked all the right questions before making a big decision, you will have an answer to those concerns when inevitably confronted. It is forgivable to be wrong, but it is not admissible to make bad decisions without first processing the possible results.

Be good at saying, "I'm sorry."
No one enjoys admitting fault. However, it is one thing to be wrong and admit error, while it's a completely different problem to be wrong and refuse to admit it. One is chalked up to humility, the other to stubbornness. A well-practiced, sincere apology merits charity for a long time.

Biblical Warning

If you want to see how young leaders should live their lives to be seen as mature, we need to look no further than Paul's writings. In 1 Timothy 4:12, we read, "Let no one despise you for your youth, but set the believers an example in speech, in conduct, in love, in faith, in purity." While not the exact purpose of this verse, there is a valuable truth that can be mined from it. How is someone young and unproven expected to earn respect and trust from those around them? By setting the example in speech, conduct, love, faith, and purity. If you can do these things early in your ministry, deserving the "big kid" label will not be something you will have to be concerned with.

CHAPTER 2

Gracefully Contend with Your Predecessor

"Blaming others takes time and energy from improving yourself."

- Anonymous -

The unfortunate legacy of the "last person" may be the reason you were hired. In fact, if you are skilled at "reading between the lines," you may have noticed some curiously specific questions or situations posited to you during your interview process. As has been the case in all of my youth ministry positions, the last person was a beloved, long-tenured, and faithful servant of the church. However, no one is perfect. In many ways, the committee who hired you is seeking to strengthen the previous leader's perceived weaknesses while simultaneously improving upon their areas of strength. That anticipates that your job comes with all sorts of lofty expectations that you may not yet comprehend. Therefore, how you "pay your respects" towards your predecessor is especially important.

There are two unhelpful ways that new (and not so new) youth directors converse about his predecessor: they look down on him or discount themselves by only looking up to his legacy. These approaches are not gracious, edifying, honest, or charitable. More specific to the habits you are trying to cultivate, neither of these endear you to the whole church. We need to realize that every church has someone who wishes that the last person was still in your position. When we choose to take either of the two aforementioned approaches, we risk developing an ungracious heart. This chapter will walk through the common pitfalls that result from these two unhelpful responses and offer some alternative replies.

Unhelpful Response 1: Looking Down on Your Predecessor

This is probably the most prevalent error that new youth directors commit regarding the person who preceded them. This is easy to do, considering that the average tenure of a youth director in America is eighteen months! The causes of these brief employments are numerous, but the result is the same: a church is once again searching for the next person, and the students are left in limbo. After this series of events, you enter the picture. The temptation is to blame your perceived lack of success on the habits and decisions of the person who came before you. Usually, you will not be left to presume those justifications for yourself. Instead, you will have many interested parents in the church, many senior citizens, and many students approach you with all the previous youth director's "errors" and "blunders." This creates an opportunity to begin heaping guilt and blame upon someone who is no longer providing youth ministry leadership at the church. Here are some popular ways youth directors do this:

"The last person created a toxic environment."
This can be a tempting allegation. When a youth director has a challenging time connecting with his students, he sometimes blames the "created environment" he inherited. Additionally,

parents, youth, and staff often affirm this suspicion. Of course, this may very well be the case! However, sowing long-lasting, fruitful seeds does not come from ruminating on another's perceived faults. Rather, it emerges from healing those relationships instead of using them as an excuse.

"The last person spent too much time playing games."
Often, a youth director is seen as the church-sanctioned dodgeball professional. We may even be viewed through the lens of a well-paid babysitter or entertainment manager. Perhaps the older generation in your church requests you "make sure you are planning on doing more than just playing games like the last guy." We will deal with the "big kid" syndrome in a later chapter, but it is important to recognize the nature of this assumption for now. Within this inference, there is the accusation of a refusal on the last person's part to invest spiritually in the students at your church. This is not to be taken lightly. Deciding to jump onto this and use it as an opportunity to blame the last person so that you might elevate yourself displays a problem. I recommend asking yourself the following questions. Did the last person actually play too many games? If so, was there a strategic rationale behind these games? In other words, did his strategy utilize games as a relational tool hoping that they would lead to discipleship opportunities? Does the person making this accusation have any real understanding of how the last person regularly executed his ministry vision? Be quick to stop your ministry from sowing seeds of blame based upon an appraisal that may not be accurate.

"The last person did not have any vision for the youth group."
Every youth director has *some* vision. They may not be able to articulate their ministry vision or present a logical strategy for their ministry. But I promise you, every youth director has a dream for what that ministry should be. If we are honest, there are aspects of our ministry vision that we do not know how to

explain or implement in our strategy perfectly. Many vision elements take both trial and error, which result in mistakes and successes. A youth director can seldom articulate and fulfill the desired goal within their first year at a church. If you decide to blame someone else for their incompetence in vision implementation, prepare to potentially be heavily criticized on yours. By being gracious toward others, you will earn grace.

Unhelpful Response 2: Discounting Yourself by Only Acknowledging Their Legacy

This is perhaps the more serious of the two approaches to take for one reason: you begin to destroy good things due to your own insecurity. I cannot think of a more damaging habit to gratify than tear down useful and quality ministry due to your own insecurities. This mindset is on the opposite end of the effective ministry spectrum. This goes beyond sowing bad seeds; it is digging up good ones. Below are several ways that we ordinarily do this:

"That's not my gifting."
This can be used as an excuse packed with spiritual honesty. Granted, most of us are not gifted equally in the same areas, and certainly, there is nothing wrong with that. In fact, the Bible refers to this in 1 Corinthians 12–20:

"There is one body, but it has many parts. But all its many parts make up one body. It is the same with Christ. We were all baptized by one Holy Spirit. And so we are formed into one body. It didn't matter whether we were Jews or Gentiles, slaves or free people. We were all given the same Spirit to drink. So the body is not made up of just one part. It has many parts. Suppose the foot says, 'I am not a hand. So I don't belong to the body.' By saying this, it cannot stop being part of the body. And suppose the ear says, 'I am not an eye. So, I don't belong to the body.' By saying this, it cannot stop being part of the body. If the whole body were an eye, how could it hear? If the whole body were an ear, how could it smell? God has placed each part in the body just as he wanted it to be. If all the parts were the same, how could there be a body? As it is, there are many parts. But there is only one body."

The church is made up of many parts that constitute one body. We are all different and always will be. However, this is not an excuse. We are called to aim to be excellent in all that we do. This may require more effort in certain areas than others. When we blame our perceptions of insufficiency on a lack of gifting, we are leaning on a crutch. I strongly advise against eliminating programs for the sole reason of gifting. Here are a few suggested solutions to implement instead:

- Enlist a volunteer who has the gifts necessary to "fill in the gaps."
- Determine to develop into that needed role.
- Discover which youth are leaders in the group and support them as they assist in that ministry element.
- Do not allow pride to stop you from calling on someone else for help.

"That program (existing or proposed) does not fit my ministry vision."
At times, this statement needs to be made. In fact, as will be argued later, a ministry vision should be what informs your strategy's programs and activities. The problem is this: if you are claiming that as an excuse to cease something of great value due to your sense of threat, then you are sowing a bad seed. Over time, your staff, parents, and students will grow weary of excuses

like this. When this happens, you may lose the trust that you previously enjoyed.

Endearing Responses to "Contending with Your Predecessor"

The Gospel calls the church to be charitable and gracious at all times. It is important to remember that we have been called to the task of shepherding and guarding the flock—particularly the teenaged "sheep." Building poor habits regarding how we contend with our predecessors exponentially affects our ability to impact our church. If one creates a culture of blame and degradation of beneficial ministry elements for the sake of pride, then one should not be surprised when they reap the blame and degradation for their own ministry. Instead of blaming the "last person," consider the alternatives:

Always give the benefit of the doubt to the last person.
Even if you are convinced that there was a lack of proper attention, being a gracious person yields gracious responses. Your church does not need yet another self-appointed critic, especially on the ministry staff.

Speak highly of the last person in public.
There will be plenty of time to have straightforward conversations about your predecessor during your time at your church. The place to have those discussions is not with your youth or within a public forum. Always take note publicly of the successes of the last person. Give credit where credit is due.

If you are able, speak to the last person shortly after taking the job.
This may be uncomfortable, but there are a few motives behind this.

- He may be able to shed some light on issues on which you are unaware.
- He may explain why they did certain things, which will help you sidestep unknown pitfalls.
- He may be able to warn you about the self-appointed critics within your new church.

If you take the time to consider and commend your predecessor's successes, you will be able to use that knowledge to your advantage in your time at your new church. There are reasons for everything, and you may realize that there are a host of less obvious reasons why people leave a church or are terminated. Sometimes a great ministry can be ruined by poor branding or the wrong spokesperson. Not everything is based on the final product. It is often the bad seeds that were sown early on from which the church and the youth director never fully healed.

What If You Follow a "Legend"?

We all know this person: single, good-looking, worked 24/7 at the church, attended every Fellowship of Christian Athletes' meeting, was the assistant coach for the baseball team (for free), and was a former four-sport high school athlete and college star! This person maintained a student ministry that exceeded all expectations for the church's size and was admired by everyone. Then one day, this person left for seminary, and the church hired you.

While the same principles above apply in this scenario, it is more critical than ever to embrace humility. At times, I have worked alongside the local "legend," and at other times, followed in their wake. The benefit of working alongside them is that you earn instant credibility as you step into their vacated role. The benefit of succeeding them is that you have a blueprint laid out that has been demonstrated successful. Embrace humility, follow their vision where possible, lead where your giftings allow, and use your unique God-given talents for the Kingdom of God.

Biblical Warning

Indicative of man's heart are Adam's words in Genesis 3:12, "The woman whom you gave to be with me, she gave me fruit of the tree, and I ate." Here, we see the first shifting of blame, the first attempt to displace guilt, the first excuse. Adam was called to be the head of his family and to lead both physically and spiritually. Due to his federal headship, Adam's sin caused the fall, not Eve's. After all, he was the one given the prohibition and commissioned with protecting and guarding the garden. It was Adam who would ultimately be held responsible.

When Adam realizes that he has failed to measure up to God's standard, he deflects the guilt; he blames Eve. Eve had come from Adam as bone of his bone and flesh of his flesh. Eve was the only fit companion whom God formed explicitly for Adam. When Adam was confronted with his guilt, he sought to divert the blame by accusing someone who had faithfully labored alongside him.

The result is not the restoration of Adam and the condemnation of Eve; rather, both were held accountable according to what was commanded of them.

Those of us in ministry can learn from this situation. We can shift the blame in this life, but we will all be held accountable in the end. Additionally, as teachers, we will be held to a higher standard. "Not many of you should become teachers, my brothers, for you know that we who teach will be judged with greater strictness" (James 3:1). We should be intentional not to deceive ourselves by placing our ministry deficiencies on someone else's shoulders.

CHAPTER 3

Establish Organization

"A schedule defends from chaos and whim. It is a net for catching days. It is a scaffolding on which a worker can stand and labor with both hands at sections of time."

- Ann Dillard -

There are two words that people use interchangeably: *disorganized* and *unorganized*. These two words may appear to be the same thing, but they are different. Unfortunately, for most youth directors, we often tend to fall somewhat into both categories. If someone is disorganized, it means that things under their oversight are "not properly planned or controlled." If one is unorganized, it means that they are messy. To be unorganized is better than to be disorganized, but to be both can be a disaster.

Disorganized and Unorganized

One way to keep the average youth ministry tenure at eighteen months is to be disorganized. Someone who is disorganized is unable to make events and programs happen effectively. This could include everything from the youth director who planned a family cookout and forgot to purchase buns to the one who planned a summer trip and overlooked booking hotel rooms for the group.

There is a difference between being messy but trusted to get the job accomplished and being disorganized and lacking your church's confidence. One creates a poor perception; the other leads to micromanaging. Sowing seeds of disorganization in your first year could lead to years of frustrating micromanagement down the road.

I remember when I was first aware of this contrast between being disorganized and unorganized. I had just pulled together a fall kickoff event to which over one hundred students attended. This event took weeks of preparation, planning, and setup. Up to that point, it was the most detailed event I had ever run. By God's grace, it was fantastic. The day following the event, I posted online a photo of my office filled to the brim with the pieces of equipment used to make that event happen. I wrote a caption to the effect of "event aftermath." I had many comments on my social media page about the event. Unfortunately, most of them said something like, "What is different about your office now than from before?" To me, that revealed the label that I had unknowingly earned. My church did not think that I was disorganized; I could get the job done. However, they most definitely recognized that I was unorganized. Years of being messy did not go overlooked. I had unknowingly sown seeds of being unorganized for so long that it took these off-the-cuff remarks to open my eyes to a perceived reality.

Here is my attempt to provide you with some helpful descriptions that should assist you in identifying where you are unorganized and disorganized:

A disorganized person does not jot down notes or tasks. Therefore...
Set reminders in your phone and organize by priority. I use the notepad app and enter every little task that needs to be accomplished for an event's success. Life can get hectic, and small details overlooked. Your memory is probably not as sharp as you believe it to be.

A disorganized person does not prioritize spending at least an hour each day in their office. Therefore...
Be in the office. In my experience, an hour is enough time to get all the little time-sensitive details of the day accomplished that tend to irritate people if not completed on time. I've learned that if I do not commit to doing this, I tend to delay tasks until they build up and become overwhelming. Spend the time in the office needed to get organized, and then go about your responsibilities away from the office.

A disorganized person neglects to check voice mails or emails in a timely fashion and forgets to call and text people back. Therefore...
Maintain empty inboxes. I leave texts, emails, and voice mails as "unread" until answered to have a constant reminder to respond. If you cannot be trusted to respond to people who have contacted you, you will be seen as disorganized.

Although a reputation of "unorganized" is better than one of "disorganized," we should still strive to avoid the unorganized label:

An unorganized person maintains a sloppy office. Therefore...
Take pride in the way in which your office is presented. For many, your office is the only impression they have of your organizational habits. Make sure it is a good one.

An unorganized person maintains a dirty and junk-filled vehicle. Therefore...
Do not be the person with the trashy interior vehicle. Students will talk about it when you give them rides, and they will tell their parents. Please take a few minutes each day to make sure your vehicle's interior is presentable.

An unorganized person allows their youth space to accumulate junk piles. Therefore...
Avoid transforming the youth space into a storage unit. Your youth facility needs to be a place that students are proud to bring their friends. Try to maintain a junkless youth space.

An unorganized person does not appear organized. Therefore...
Avoid being disheveled in appearance. This may seem odd, but the way you put yourself together contributes to this label. Do you always look "thrown together" in your appearance, or do you look put together? Half untucked shirts, messy and unkempt hair, or sloppy jeans will work against your desired appearance as an organized ministry leader.

These labels are easy to acquire. There are so many ways in which one can be viewed as disorganized or unorganized. Although I personally did not have the more damaging label of "disorganized," I had still encouraged a narrative that was not helpful.

Here is the sneaky thing with sowing seeds of disorganization early on: people forgive you, but only for a while. When you first begin as a youth minister, you are in the "honeymoon" phase. Almost everything is forgivable because everything is new for you and them. Mistakes are expected. But once that newness wears off, the expectations are for you to know better. Therefore, any perceived disorganized action from that time on suddenly becomes lumped together with the "honeymoon" phase mistakes, painting a potential death knell narrative about you. Sowing seeds of disorganization early on can have devastating effects down the road.

The label of "unorganized" is not as bad as that of "disorganized," but neither label is one which we should seek to claim. One of our desires as youth directors should be to remove any habits or patterns that affect our ability to do ministry well. Besides being helpful habits for your ministry, remembering the things listed above are healthy physically and psychologically. Sowing seeds of organization in the first year of ministry leads to trust and confidence in your ability to run your future ministry effectively.

Junk Accumulation

Here are some common ways in which youth directors are notorious for accumulating junk:

Storage closets
This is easy to do. Youth directors are constantly on the move, returning from trips and events late at night and needing room to off-load the van and bus at 11 p.m. Nevertheless, critical eyes inevitably notice those storage closets at the worst possible times. Devise a system to clean those closets routinely.

The youth refrigerator
Throw away what you cannot eat or send it home with students. Moldy pizza, spoiled salad dressings, and sour tea can produce a narrative about your cleanliness that you do not want.

The "guilt collection"
It never fails: Someone will think that their parent's couch from 1984 would be a perfect fit for the youth space. Or maybe it is a coffee table that weighs a ridiculous amount and belongs on a

shag carpet. In both situations, the donors genuinely mean well and trust that their offer will serve the youth ministry well. Thus, you will inevitably encounter a situation in which you will have to look at someone who is genuinely offering something kind and tell them, "No, thank you." If you cannot graciously decline things that do not fit your space, you will end up with an entire "guilt collection" of items that will be an eyesore in your ministry.

Biblical Warning

The Bible does not speak about returning text messages or maintaining a tidy office. You will not find a verse that explains the value of rejecting hand-me-down furniture. However, you will find verses that speak of hard work and attention to detail. Much of what was discussed in this chapter has to do with hard work. Attention to small details requires extra work on our part.

> "The ants are not a strong people, but they pre-
> pare their food in the summer;"
> —Proverbs 30:25

> "Poor is he who works with a negligent hand,
> But the hand of the diligent makes rich."
> —Proverbs 10:4

> "Good planning and hard work lead to prosperity,
> but hasty shortcuts lead to poverty."
> —Proverbs 21:5

When disorganized and unorganized, we take time and effectiveness away from the students in whom we have been called to invest. Develop a system that increases your effectiveness!

CHAPTER 4

Rally Volunteers

"We can find meaning and reward by serving some higher purpose than ourselves, a shining purpose, the illumination of a thousand points of light."
- George H. W. Bush -

Ministry was never intended to be a solo affair. Thus, the "CEO" pastor is not a model that I believe can be defended with Scripture. Rather, pastors should serve alongside other ministers and elders. The same should be expected from us in our youth ministries. This means we should be intentional when it comes to recruiting volunteers. I have three main reasons why your first year will be your best chance to effectively engage volunteers in your ministry. First, almost everyone will be interested in the direction that the "new person" has in mind. Second, new is exciting, and many people like to be a part of something new. Third, you have not had time to make anyone angry enough to write you off! With that in mind, rallying volunteers should be a primary focus during your first year, considering the energy is generally in your favor.

As we advance, we will focus on the process of volunteer recruitment. As it is with all ministry elements, no "cookie-cutter" approach works for everyone. However, some general principles should at least be acknowledged. There are three stages to building a healthy volunteer base: recruitment, safety, and training.

Recruitment

Listed below are five suggestions for effective volunteer recruitment. Every church has its own variables and concerns that can make recruiting volunteers challenging. However, I believe the recommendations listed below apply to every church:

1. "Sell" the Vision (Chapter 11) and the Strategy (Chapter 12).

There is a certain level of skill required to stand before a crowd of people and articulate your vision in a way that provokes excitement and energy. This takes practice, presence, and confidence. Before you ask for volunteers, commit time to crafting and wording your ministry vision and strategy in a captivating and inspirational manner.

2. Present the need for volunteers in an appealing manner.

People are busy. In fact, I am often surprised by how engaged many people are in their church. For many, it is like a second job. I believe that this speaks to the prominent role that the local church should have in her members' lives. However, we also live in what has been labeled "the busiest time in history." Convincing people to volunteer their limited evenings and weekends for your ministry often requires discernible conviction on their part. Your job in volunteer recruitment is to know best how to communicate that need.

3. Be specific.

Vagueness limits your pool of volunteers. Many men and women in the church will not volunteer because they feel as if they are not qualified to lead a small group. However, if they heard that you were searching for volunteers to cook for the youth, assist with carpool, or enforce crowd control, you may find you have more volunteers than you know what to do with! Be specific in your needs so your church members can evaluate where they belong.

4. Be intentional about asking.
Do not shy away from asking a direct question. People are often waiting for the personal invite because it assures them that you want their help.

5. Ask your colleagues at the church to review volunteers' names before you commit them to a permanent role.
Since you are new, it is important to hear other staff's wisdom on your potential volunteers. They can inform you of any concerns (bad habits, loose tongue, overcommitted, etc.) that may help later on. Additionally, they may also contribute some other names that may fit within your ministry plan.

Safety

Another essential aspect of a healthy volunteer base is safety. Sadly, we live in a time where some individuals cannot be trusted around children. I would advise looking into a service that provides criminal background checks and utilize their services annually.

There should also be a strict and agreed-upon list of boundaries between youth and adults. These boundaries should include things such as: one-on-one time, text and phone conversations, and social media interactions. A quick Google search will find all sorts of "best practices" lists to help create the precautions. I highly recommend having each volunteer read and sign a document that acknowledges the seriousness of these rules which you disseminate. Your church may already have a stated set of "best practice" rules in place, so be sure to check with church leadership. Creating a high standard of safety expectations should help in the following ways:

It will demonstrate to the parents that you are concerned about their children's safety.
Parents need to know that you think like an adult (see "Big Kid" chapter) and have their children's best interests in mind at all times. Prove that you are concerned about the safety of their children just as much as they are.

It will serve as a potential roadblock to anyone with sinister intentions.
Historically, churches are easy targets for child predators, and we have to work with this disturbing truth in mind. Having consistent, accountable standards for adults and minors will help prevent opportunities for people with perverse motives.

It protects both you and the church legally.
It is sad that we have to think like this, but it is the age we live in. Sometimes, despite best practices, bad things happen. By having the proper systems in place, you will protect the church legally so that a lawsuit does not shutter its doors.

Are Background Checks Really Necessary?

This is one of those tasks that are often ignored in "friendly-face" ministry. The "friendly-face ministry" is a ministry that ignores best practices for minors because the volunteers are well-known and appear to be honorable people. And this is usually the case. However, studies show that 90% of abuse victims know their abuser[1] and that in 60% of those cases, the abuser was

---

1. Finkelhor, D. (2012). *Characteristics of Crimes against Juveniles*. Durham, NH: Crimes against Children Research Center.

trusted by the family[2]. As leaders to whom parents entrust their children, we have every responsibility to do our due diligence to protect our students physically and emotionally. Several services work with churches in this area, and some of these can be found listed in the appendix. Be warned; there is no "silver bullet" for this issue. According to MinistrySafe.com (a great service for churches):

- More than 90% of sexual abusers have no criminal record to find, and they know it.
- Teen abusers have no searchable criminal records because juvenile records are generally unavailable.
- Sexual abuse offenders are often allowed to "plea down" to a lesser offense, such that a background check may reveal lesser offenses that may not alert untrained personnel to the dangerous nature of an applicant's past behavior.

Identifying people who have unethical intentions is not always easy. Still, the church has the moral (and legal) responsibility to be equipped, trained, and prepared to protect the students who participate in their ministries. Here are a few rules that you can implement with your volunteers that will serve as guardrails for your students and volunteers:

No communication after 7:00 p.m.
I have yet to meet the parent that is thrilled that their teenage daughter is texting a male volunteer late into the night. The best practice for everyone is to be sure that parents never feel like conversations are happening behind their backs.

---

2. Whealin, J. (2007-05-22). "Child Sexual Abuse". National Center for Post Traumatic Stress Disorder, US Department of Veterans Affairs.

Volunteers can NEVER promise "not to tell."
There are two fundamental reasons for this. First, ministry leaders and volunteers certainly have a responsibility to preserve the integrity of the relationship with the students. However, they have a higher responsibility to protect the student's physical and spiritual well-being. There have been many times I have had to discuss with parents the details of private conversations I had with their child. There are both legal and moral reasons for this. Second, if a teenager feels as if they have some level of protection for what they say, there is a higher chance of inappropriate exchanges between the student and volunteer. Volunteers must always be seen as leaders, and by promising "not to tell," volunteers lower themselves to that of a peer.

Why Train Volunteers?

From a strategic perspective, one of the most detrimental mistakes a youth director can make with volunteers is to thrust them into roles that they have not been properly trained to undertake. There is a wealth of resources that can be accessed for free and some established programs that you can purchase and use to do this effectively. My goal in this section is to shed light on the dangers of enabling an untrained volunteer in your youth ministry:

An untrained volunteer is an unknown liability.
If you have not spent the time investing in and training your volunteers, you will not accurately gauge their strengths and weaknesses. You will also be unable to see how the students interact with that leader until you (and they) are already committed. This leader then becomes a liability because you have no true judgment of their passion, responsibility, or maturity.

An untrained volunteer may not speak the language.
When students have issues about some ministry vision element, they often go to a volunteer with their concerns. If your volunteers have not been trained on the vision, strategy, and importance of your ministry's various aspects, they may unknowingly undercut your authority out of sheer ignorance. Volunteers need to learn the language to be a unified team focused on the same goal.

An untrained volunteer is an unaccountable volunteer.
If someone has never been given a job description, then it is difficult to hold them accountable for a job poorly (or never) done. If your volunteers are untrained, then it will not only be challenging for them to achieve the standard you expect, but it will be frustrating for you to enforce a standard of which they are unaware.

An untrained volunteer feels lost.
Some volunteers feel self-conscious around a group of teenagers. You are accustomed to it, and they are not. Throwing them into the mix without the needed training and preparation is a guaranteed way to make a volunteer feel as if they are left to figure it out on their own. Once they come to this conclusion, their commitment to your ministry may drop, their passion may fade, and they may become an ineffective volunteer that you now have to try to manage.

Training a volunteer takes both time and energy, both of which are finite resources. Nonetheless, make it a priority to train your volunteers and set a fair expectation for their investment in your ministry. If their training is important to you, your ministry will become that much more important to them.

Broaden Your Volunteer Horizons

It is easy to become comfortable with your volunteer group. This is a good thing. We should want to have great relationships with those who are helping. However, there is a danger in surrounding ourselves only with those who are familiar to us. Recall King Rehoboam in 1 Kings 12. In the story, the people of Israel requested that the new king lessen their burdens, for his father put a heavy yoke upon them. King Rehoboam consulted his friends, who had grown up serving with him, and the elders. The wisdom of the elders called for the king to be lenient. The advice of Rehoboam's friends was to double down. King Rehoboam received the counsel of his friends and increased the burden upon the people.

The danger that Rehoboam faced is one that you may also face: always listening to familiar voices. Therefore, be sure to incorporate new voices and new personalities into your ministry. Allow other parents and adults to serve and minister alongside you. Encourage a diverse network of volunteers so that you do not end like the Old Testament king, disliked by everyone outside of his "clique."

Biblical Warning

As mentioned at the beginning of the chapter, there is a clear biblical precedent for surrounding yourself with other leaders who can help in the ministry's work. One place that especially feels like youth ministry to me is when the Israelites are grumbling to Moses in the desert. This story seems so relatable to a youth director because the Israelites complained about food and water. In Moses's frustration, he appeals to the Lord for help.

In Numbers 11:16, we read, "16Then the Lord said to Moses, 'Gather for me seventy men of the elders of Israel, whom you know to be the elders of the people and officers over them, and bring them to the tent of meeting, and let them take their stand there with you.'"

God's response to Moses displayed understanding and concern. God commanded Moses to surround himself with godly men who could assist Moses in the spiritual leadership of Israel. Search for volunteers who fit this criteria.

CHAPTER 5

Prove You Are Teachable

"Be willing to be a beginner every single morning."
- Meister Eckhart -

Ministry is personal. When youth directors have weak elements in their ministry, or their strategy appears to be faulty, oversight and critique can be interpreted as a personal attack. Instead of responding thoughtfully, we tend to respond emotionally. But, as ministry leaders, we should accept critique from the perspective of a consultant, not from that of a content creator. We need to remove any emotional ties to what is being critiqued and seek to form an unbiased opinion. In other words, accept critique and criticism as constructive, not pejorative.

In the hit comedy show *The Office*, Michael Scott is the Regional Manager of a floundering, "mid-level" paper company in Scranton, Pennsylvania. The character of Michael Scott is routinely hysterical, offensive, comical, loving, and cringeworthy . . . sometimes all at the same time! In the Season 2 "Performance Review" episode, Michael asks his staff to use the Suggestion Box on the wall so that he could get everyone's "Constructive Compliments." Kelly, from the Customer Service Department, corrects him by pointing out that he meant to say

"Constructive Criticism," which in itself was a criticism. Michael was not impressed.

You see, for Michael Scott, everything is personal: employees, employers, business, paper, and opinions. This is a character flaw that makes him lovable, comical, and annoying. Unfortunately, this is a similar flaw that we see in many ministry leaders. And in real life, this flaw is much less lovable and comical than it is in a TV show.

I recommend a shift in perspective: Instead of receiving criticism as the content creator, we should welcome criticism from the perspective of a consultant. A consultant is brought in to evaluate a situation, hear varying opinions, and make unbiased decisions. A consultant's goal is to help make that company, ministry, or relationship better through a constructive change. A consultant possesses a judgment that disregards emotions so that he can clearly communicate the next step forward. Often, the critiques are painful to hear (think Gordon Ramsey on *Kitchen Nightmares*).

Contrast the role of a consultant with that of a creator. The creator's job is to make what he feels to be the best possible product and then defend and explain his rationale afterward. The creator isn't really in the business of providing critique: He is in the business of defending his creation. He is patently biased. His work is unavoidably personal. And this isn't necessarily a bad thing! This becomes a bad thing when these biases function as blinders.

Admittedly, not every commentary will be constructive or helpful. However, if ministry leaders feel personally attacked by critique and only desire to receive "Michael Scott constructive compliments," then they are likely not teachable. Let us decide now to welcome critique as consultants.

I find that youth directors are often spinning their wheels in a frivolous attempt to demonstrate that they are adults and should be taken seriously. Since there are many unhelpful labels that youth ministry has (unfortunately) earned, youth directors often enter a new church with the deck stacked against them. Of course, as we have already discussed, much of this is their own doing by being undisciplined when it comes to demonstrating a mature heart and mind. The result is a hardening of and a doubling down on the part of these youth directors, who are resolved to continue on their chosen path and to prove that they are right. This coincides with the aforementioned description of a biased creator, and it is not a helpful approach.

Hall of Fame basketball coach John Wooden once said, "It's what you learn after you know it all that counts." Teachability is more than being capable of being taught; it is being willing and excited to learn. One cannot be willing to be taught unless they have first learned to be both humble and honest about themselves. Here are six attributes of a teachable heart for you to consider:

1. Being teachable means listening with as little bias as you can marshal.

This is perhaps the most difficult aspect of a teachable heart because it requires the listener to "check his ego at the door." You cannot bring your defenses and arguments into the conversation until you have listened with an open, charitable, and willing heart. Think like a consultant, not a creator.

2. Being teachable means embracing correction.

There will be times in your ministry where you are faced with a situation that you felt you handled flawlessly. However, others will wholeheartedly disagree with your analysis. You have two options at this point: argue your point or make a correction from the point of view of a consultant. Defensiveness can strain relationships, which will affect both you and your ministry. I am not proposing you walk around waving a white flag, but embracing correction means removing your pride from the equation.

3. Being teachable means searching for critique.

This is something that many youth directors avoid. At my current employment, we evaluate our ministry every year, attempting to see what is ineffective, what could be done better, what we need to add, or what we need to eliminate. Regular opportunities for evaluation are healthy and will help avoid a surprise bombardment of built-up frustration by a parent, student, or leader. Find people who will give honest feedback regarding your ministry and then analyze the data.

4. Being teachable means admitting fault.

If you cannot admit your mistakes, then you cannot claim to be teachable. Be honest about your faults and seek forgiveness when it is called for.

5. Being teachable means learning from your mistakes.

It is not enough to merely recognize errors in our ministries, but we must attempt to improve them. If you forget to send out a packing list for a trip, you should make it a point never to make that same mistake again. Repeated mistakes mature into bad habits, and bad habits produce the narrative that you are unteachable.

6. Being teachable means being aware of your limitations.

Based on my experience, youth directors tend to be fairly confident people. Because of this, they are eager to take a big gamble or commit heavy time investment in an event or program. It is wise to listen to those around you who do not have their perspective clouded by the excitement of a new idea. These people will also have an honest perspective on your strengths and weaknesses, informing their judgment of your limitations.

I'm convinced that if you can take these attributes of teach-ability and apply them to your ministry in your first year, you will see long-lasting success in your ministry.

Community

One of the most difficult lessons to learn is the value of a pro-fessional community. For the sake of this section, I am consider-ing "professional community" to be a group of other youth work-ers who are laboring in the same ministry context as you (city, county, or state). Often, youth directors find themselves feeling isolated in their ministry capacity. The result of an isolated youth director is that the only professional voice speaking into his min-istry is his own. This means that local experiences of both failure and success within his professional community are absent. This is a dangerous place to reside. Ministry in an echo chamber lacks the influence to succeed. Below are some reasons to seek a pro-fessional community in youth ministry:

Community provides perspective.
As stated before, perspective is important. It is of considerable value to analyze your situation and your community's situation from the perspective of a fresh pair of youth ministry eyes.

Community helps you see the shared battles every youth di-rector is fighting.
Isolation can lead to hopelessness. Youth workers can begin to feel as if they are fighting an uphill battle by themselves. This is especially true if they feel as if their church is not providing the necessary support structure. A professional community works positively against this psychological feeling of loneliness that of-ten accompanies youth ministry.

Community provides you with fresh ideas.
Most of my ideas have not originated from a place of single imaginings. In reality, I tend to observe something that sparks an idea within me. It is almost as if I see a thread and begin to pull, only to find out that the thread is part of something larger. A professional community should do this for all of us in youth ministry; it supplies a common cultural context to evaluate, share, and develop our ideas.

Community lays claim to what has not succeeded.
Investing in the youth ministry professional community will allow a youth director to learn what has and, equally important, has not worked in the past. This is vital information for a new youth director to secure. However, just because it has worked in the past for you at another church does not mean it will work in your new ministry context.

Community creates competition.
Competition in ministry can be poisonous. There can at times, however, be great value in being pushed by your youth ministry colleagues. It is tempting to find a smooth-running strategy and grow complacent. Learning what other youth ministries in your area are doing should inspire you to "up your game" to stay sharp, fresh, and ultimately, relevant. Use your professional community to push you to be effective and intentional in discipling a new generation of Christians within your city.

"Local Color"

Local color is defined as "the customs, manner of speech, dress, or other typical features of a place or period that contribute to its particular character." What is the "local color" of your church? There is a fine line between using local culture and allowing current culture to use you. I once heard it said that, "Culture defines our context, not our content." Hence, it is essential to understand the context in which we minister. In New Orleans, churches need to understand what happens when Mardi Gras comes around, whereas churches in Bismarck probably do not. The people in Bismarck have other, more relevant local cultural priorities. Culture will be different in every location, and it is material during your first year at a new church to begin to learn and understand that culture before making any major shifts. Here are some ways to begin to understand the culture in your area:

Find out what sport teams your church members follow.
If you minister in Lubbock, you are going to have a lot of Red Raider fans. If you minister in Jacksonville, you will have a church full of Gators fans. Identifying these things allows you to learn what is culturally "sacred" and what is not.

Learn your church members' hobbies.
What do your members do for fun? Are they hobbies that you can share with them and use as relation-building activities?

Go to high school extracurriculars.
If you want to know what is important to your students and their parents, see what their school values are. Do they have a large high school football culture? If so, perhaps a fall retreat is not the best idea.

Listen to the advice of your church.
Great ideas with poor timing become bad ideas all the time. This means that once you have failed due to an incomplete perception

of your church culture, you will have a difficult time in the future achieving the necessary traction to attempt that idea again.

Culture in General

The challenge that any church faces regarding culture is deciding where to draw the line. What is the line between cave in to culture and standing opposed to it? When are we losing the uniqueness of the message of the church, and when are we engaging the culture for Christ? I have a few thoughts on this:

When we jeopardize the purity of the Gospel, we cave in to culture.
The undiluted truth of the Gospel is what will win others for Christ every time. Refusing to address sin in our culture does no favors to anyone. Love requires discipline (Hebrews 12:5–8; Proverbs 6:23)

When we sacrifice the priority of the Gospel, we cave in to culture.
Some churches cancel services for some of the worldly reasons. What message are we putting forth to the world when we allow culture to take precedent over our weekly worship?

Embrace culture when it parallels God's Word.
I see much value in using culture when it falls in line with God's Word. Participate in community family days, join fundraising events, assist in humanitarian aid, but always do these things with the lens of Christ in focus.

Do not let culture determine your content.
Being a minister to God's people requires the ability to speak the truth at all times. We are more than role models and more than friends. We are ministers called to proclaim the truth of God's Word.

God has placed you in your specific circumstances for a reason. Russel Moore wrote, "To rail against the culture is to say to God that we are entitled to a better mission field than the one he has given us."[3] Maybe you are left to share in the sorrowful work of "the weeping prophet" Jeremiah, or maybe God has placed you in a field that is ripe for harvest. Either way, ministering in discontent will be a fruitless labor.

In Romans 12:2, Paul warns us, "Do not be conformed to this world, but be transformed by the renewal of your mind, that by testing you may discern what is the will of God, what is good and acceptable and perfect." As such, the church is to have a different mindset than that of the world. We are to be transformed in a manner that causes us to look like Jesus rather than the society around us. Conforming to the world is the opposite of conforming to Christ.

Listen to Your Spouse

I am not of the mindset that when a church hires a youth director, they also hire the spouse. However, I am of the mindset that one's spouse should be actively invested in the ministry of their husband or wife.

My wife is the anchor for my mental health in ministry. She provides space to vent, complain, debate, lament, cheer, and be excited about every aspect of ministry. She deals graciously with my absence during youth trips, late-night activities, and online video game sessions with the youth. She tolerates my chaotic schedule (which is anything but a routine 9–5) and is prepared to follow the calling God has placed in my heart. She is in every way a partner in ministry, even though she is not laboring in the youth room alongside me.

---

3. Moore, R. (2015). Onward: Engaging the culture without losing the gospel. Nashville, TN: B & H Pub. Group. Pg. 181

With that in mind, no one knows me better. No one has a better feel for when I need to say "no," when I need to apologize, or when I need to draw some important boundaries. Your spouse is your partner in ministry, even if they are not actively working alongside you. Because of this, we need to hear what our spouses have to say, and we need to value their concerns. Teachability extends to our relationship with our spouses.

Biblical Warning

Humility and teachability are foundational aspects of godly character. Even Jesus spent his younger years submitting to his parents and at the temple, discussing and learning from the resident rabbis. Learning is not just for the young and young at heart. Rather, it is a continual process that should never end.

1 Peter 5:5 tells us this, "In the same way, you who are younger, submit yourselves to your elders. All of you, clothe yourselves with humility toward one another, because 'God opposes the proud, but shows favor to the humble.'" One can only learn if he is humble, and one can only be humble if he believes he still has much to learn. Surround yourself with people who can teach you.

CHAPTER 6

Seek to be Well-Rounded

*"The main purpose of education isn't just to receive
a certification that leads to a career, but to become a
well-rounded person in so many aspects of life."*
- Edmond Mbiaka -

To be "well-rounded" means that one is: well-read, well-experienced, and well-trained. Your church hired you to be the resident expert on teenagers, therefore, set your focus on being just that. The only way to do this is by staying current with teenage culture, as well as advancing in your overall expertise in ministry. Commit to being a well-rounded youth minister early in your time at your church.

Well-Read

Overall, the perceived value of a well-read person is no longer appreciated. Because of this, there is a tendency for youth directors to lean overmuch on the internet as their primary resource for ministry. While the internet is an abundant source of knowledge, it is often unvetted. I believe that having the "vetted" resources on your shelves and the online content you trust are the best approaches. That being said, here are some tips for being well-read:

Being well-read means you can lean on the wisdom of others.
There is genuine relief that one feels when he can back up his ideas by credible research and sources. Stating "I think" may feel good when you are right, but saying "research shows" is often best.

Being well-read shows others you have done your research.
Parents want to know that your ministry practice is up to date. By referring to studies, examples, or professional publications, you can assure them that what may become adjustments of ministerial direction are more than whimsical changes.

Being well-read allows you to recognize current trends.
If one is aware of past trends and strategies, they can see when they became irrelevant and how students reacted to those strategies. Once one has that knowledge, they can identify the new movements before they happen. A classic example is that of the "Event-Run Youth Ministry" model. This model was simple: blow it out and blow it out big. When iPhones, social media, and other entertainment options increased in America in the late 90s, this model began to die. Instead, students sought genuine community through small groups and personal discipleship because that was what students were missing. Youth ministers who noticed the trends shifting did well to alter course accordingly.

Well-Experienced

Being well-experienced does not mean having a testimony detailed with a host of horrific sins that enables you to connect with the students. To consider someone as being "well-experienced," I would want them to have a broad appreciation of many life interests. Although fun and useful as a time to unwind, video games should not comprise the totality of one's hobbies. Here are some thoughts:

Find a primary hobby.
Everyone needs an outlet, so choose one that is edifying.

Be able to talk about a wide variety of topics.
There is a term for someone who can "do it all:" *Renaissance man.* This is one who is educated enough in his life and scholastics to have substantial conversations about a plethora of subjects. Work to broaden your horizons by reading from a variety of reputable resources each week.

Experience what other ministries are currently doing.
Take a handful of evenings each year and attend other youth ministry events to see how they function and connect with their students. If you have a friend doing ministry in another city, take the opportunity to watch them work and pick their brain.

Well-Trained

In many professional fields in the country, employees have mandatory training and continuing education required by their employers. For some reason, youth directors have difficulty obtaining the budget or time to make a yearly training conference a reality. Here are some tips to accomplish this important goal:

Request a yearly continuing education budget early.
The best time to request continuing education funding is during the hiring process. This accomplishes three things. First, it shows your wisdom in seeking to invest in yourself in a way that will benefit the church. This demonstrates maturity. Second, including this in the hiring conditions causes it to be more difficult to trim from the budget later. Since this was not a youth budget

issue, but rather part of your employment terms, the continuing education designation usually remains. Third, it shows a willingness to learn, a humility that allows for one to be taught, and an eagerness to always bring the best out of yourself for your new church.

Have a detailed plan for the funds.

Be specific enough to merit the trust of the people who control the finances by informing them of your goals. You may have a vision for how you will receive your training, but they may need to have more information than simply "continuing ed." Present a specific conference option, along with the travel estimates, lodging, and book costs.

Identify the important issues on the horizon that require training.

When explaining the need for continuing education and training, be able to point to specific concerns on the horizon for which you feel the need to be prepared. What are those threats, shifts, or cultural concerns on the horizon that you need to be equipped to address with confidence? How does this conference or training bolster you regarding these concerns?

In my experience, well-rounded youth directors are difficult to obtain. Set a precedent in your first year at your new church as a well-rounded minister. Work diligently to become the resident expert on teenagers that they expect you to be.

Defeating Laziness

Much of the work done by a youth director can go unrecognized. Often, this is because much of what we do is outside of the church's brick-and-mortar boundaries. This can often lead to a long leash and a lack of accountability. This opens the door for a danger that can easily sneak into our lives: laziness. Why should we truly be concerned with laziness?

Laziness is difficult to admit to.
Most people do not believe that they are lazy. In my experience, I only recognize that I have been lazy after other people have been noticing it for a while. Because we are familiar with the irregular hours and unnoticed workload, we are quick to defend our time use and perceived workload. This makes admitting to laziness even more difficult.

Laziness is sneaky.
Some ministers are unable to see their own laziness. Early in my marriage, I owned a landscape company. I would wake up, check the weather, and call off work if there were any chance of rain. I did not qualify this as laziness as much as I did foresight. Beware of laziness parading as foresight.

Laziness is sinful.
We do not often think of laziness as a sin, but it is. Proverbs 6:9–12 says, "9How long will you lie there, you sluggard? When will you get up from your sleep? 10A little sleep, a little slumber, a little folding of the hands to rest—11and poverty will come on you like a thief and scarcity like an armed man. 12A troublemaker and a villain, who goes about with a corrupt mouth." Again, in Colossians 3:23, we read, "Whatever you do, work at it with all your heart, as working for the Lord, not for human masters." We are called to be diligent laborers in the field that God has set before us; to do anything else is sinful.

Tips for Defeating Laziness

Nicolas Cole, a contributing author for Inc.com, wrote a piece in 2016 called, "8 Habits of the Most Successful People that Lazy

People Lack."[4] You can find the entire article cited in the appendix, but I will give you his eight points in brief:

1. Successful people plan ahead.
2. Successful people do the hard stuff first.
3. Successful people say no.
4. Successful people invest in themselves.
5. Successful people surround themselves with other successful people.
6. Successful people study their craft.
7. Successful people are accountable for their actions.
8. Successful people believe in themselves.

Situate yourself so that your normal routine and habits actively fight against the ministry-stunting sin of laziness. If you routinely find a large amount of free time on your hands, make use of the "Defeating Laziness Idea Prompts" in the appendix.

Be Above Reproach

It is important to be seen as "above reproach" in every aspect of our lives. According to an article by Rev. Steven Koster for Familyfire.com, "Clergy abuse is remarkably common—in one study, 12% of pastors admitted to having sex with a parishioner, and only 23% of victims ever reported misconduct to church officials."[5] This should be a sobering statistic that youth directors, and all ministry leaders for that matter, earnestly heed. The temptation for ministry leaders is great and has devastating ramifications.

---

4. See Appendix
5. Garland, D. R. (2006). "When Wolves Wear Shepherds' Clothing: Helping Women Survive Clergy Sexual Abuse." Retrieved from https://www.nacsw .org/Publications/GarlandArticle.pdf

Titus 1:7–9 says, "For an overseer, as God's steward, must be above reproach. He must not be arrogant or quick-tempered or a drunkard or violent or greedy for gain, but hospitable, a lover of good, self-controlled, upright, holy, and disciplined." Not only are we to refrain from "big sins" like sexual misconduct, but we are to be "above reproach" in everything. Our actions and decisions must not only be pure, but they must be perceived as pure. This goes for more than just relationships, but such things as finances and church equipment. Being "above reproach" means that we work diligently not to allow ourselves to be vulnerable for accusation. Here are some ways to do just that:

Never be alone with a student.

I understand that this can be difficult. We seem always to have a student that requires a ride home or whose parents are the last to pick them up. In light of that, do your best to arrange for another adult to wait with you or join you on the drop-off trip. Particularly, I would advise against being alone in a car with a student of the opposite sex.

Avoid being overly informal with students.

Avoid becoming too informal with the students. Yes, you should be a friend and a role model. But you are also an authority figure. On the one hand, becoming too informal can lead to a false perception of infatuation or romantic feelings, which is especially dangerous. On the opposite hand, students without this perceived "extra" attention from you may feel isolated and less connected than other students.

Do not accept cash without another adult present as a witness.

I cannot begin to count the number of times a student has handed me cash for trips. Always make sure another adult witnesses the exchange and that the cash is submitted to the finance department ASAP.

Track your hours.
Periodically, I take a few weeks out of the quarter to track my hours. I do this for two reasons: to hold myself accountable and to have something to show when questioned about my hours, location, or ethics. Doing this will also show you where you need to pick up the slack and where you might consider easing up.

Biblical Warning

King David's great sin was one that came from a lack of accountability. If you remember the story, it begins with the line, "In the spring of the year, the time when kings go out to battle, David sent Joab, and his servants with him, and all Israel. And they ravaged the Ammonites and besieged Rabbah. But David remained at Jerusalem" (2 Samuel 11:1). When David should have been at war, leading his people, he remained home. In the privacy of his palace he saw, lusted after, and committed adultery with Bathsheba. Additionally, he ordered that Bathsheba's husband, Uriah, was to be exposed and left for dead by the army. The seemingly minor lack of accountability had devastating ramifications.

Temptation lies in wait for lack of accountability. Be careful not to allow the freedom and trust that your church has in you lead to sin.

CHAPTER 7

Take Charge of Your Time

"Having healthy boundaries not only requires being able to say "no," but also being willing and able to enforce that "no" when necessary."
- Jessica Moore -

Many leaders have difficulty in their ministry context when it comes to declining extra tasks or projects. I believe this is particularly the case for the youth director because he is uniquely positioned between ministries, unlike many other staff members. Youth ministry manages to bleed over into children's, young adult, and college ministries. As such, when there are service projects around the church community or church itself (that are no doubt low-hanging fruit), the teenagers are oftentimes the first to be volunteered. Adding to this, the youth director is often one of the younger staff members. When IT issues arise, they are often one of the first people charged with providing wanted assistance. Overall, the youth director can easily turn into the church "Swiss Army knife," soon becoming an overworked and overloaded man or woman.

Due to the nature of a youth minister's calling, many often have difficulty responding "no." By definition, *ministry* is a call-

ing of service, and when the flock needs help, we feel the obliga-
tion to respond. This is a noble and true role of pastoral ministry
that should not be dismissed. Granted, one should endeavor to
be as valuable to their new church as possible. However, we must
become experts at discerning ministry tasks from non-ministry
tasks, evaluating our current time investment, and distinguishing
priorities. We are called, first and foremost, to minister to students. If student ministry suffers due to additional, nonessential
tasks, then we may experience failure. Recognizing when to say
"no" is critical for a long and healthy ministry experience. The
following are questions to ask yourself to assist in easily identifying priorities:

Does this task fall within the bounds of your job description?
If at all possible, request a job description. A well-constructed
job description will provide boundaries, as well as communicate
expectations of which you were unaware.

**Are you meeting your expected time commitment as a youth
minister?**
Is the church receiving what they are paying for? If you are full-
time, are you genuinely fulfilling the 35–40 hours per/week
commitment, or are you routinely falling short? As often seems
to be the plight of part-time youth workers, are you currently
working 30 hours and only getting paid for 20? An honest evaluation of your time commitment is a significant filter to employ.

**Is the requested task of a higher priority than your regular
duties?**
There will be occasions when the church's higher good must
come before your "normal" responsibilities. Is there help needed
with Vacation Bible School decorations or a church workday in
which you should participate? Taking these questions into consideration, sometimes the only deciding factor is the overall pri-

ority of the task. Church-wide priorities should outrank that of individual ministries.

Is anyone else capable of doing the job?

This is a question of wise delegation. Early in my ministry, I remember when the youth committee encouraged me to delegate busy-work errands or routine facility maintenance to a volunteer or intern. The justification was that I was hired to prioritize ministry according to a skill set unique to myself, which was hindered by a commitment of large amounts of time to errands. Granted, the tasks needed to be accomplished. However, there was a more advantageous way to manage my time by practicing wise delegation. As a warning, be careful not to confuse delegation with laziness. Wise delegation will be applauded. Laziness, on the other hand, will be recognized for precisely what it is.

Is this a one-time task, or are you committing yourself indefinitely?

Be cautious when committing yourself to open-ended projects. If you pledge to do a task, do so with the caveat of a definite but gracious deadline. You can always choose to help past the deadline if time permits, but it establishes an expectation of completion from the start.

Does this task further ministry, friendship, or both?

Often, we do things, even when we feel we do not possess the time, because it advances our ministry efforts. We do other tasks because they act as a bridge to relationships with students. But, sometimes, these relationships can stretch our time commitment beyond what is practical. Evaluate the fruitfulness of your time in this regard.

Have a justified motivation for saying "no."

It is important to have substantial grounds for declining a new task. Principally, we should strive to be honest and willing servants of the church. However, it is important that whoever is asking you also has a strong case for why they believe you should be the one to help. When possible, it is helpful to cite specific reasons for declining to avoid the appearance of laziness or indifference.

Do not accept tasks with the private purpose of leveraging them for a future pay raise.

Be careful leveraging your negligence to say "no" to voluntary tasks against your desire for increased compensation. Not only is this, at the core, an unbiblical approach, but it often leads to a possible "red flag" for church leadership. The extra tasks may raise the question of whether or not you have been neglecting your primary purpose at church: youth ministry.

Be in constant, honest dialogue over this subject with your pastor and committee members.

The staff members whom you serve alongside face the same quandary. Each of you is answering a call to ministry. There is always more work to be done than people. The best way to avoid burnout and overcommitment is through clear and open communication.

Paying attention to these priority-evaluating questions will help you take charge of your time. It is important to note that recognizing when to say "no" is always a matter of discernment. This is a lesson that I have learned the hard way. I have loved the churches at which I have served, and I am passionate about my calling. My passion for the local church inclines me to take on added tasks that would cost the church extra funds to outsource. A hard lesson learned was this: By taking on extra duties that were not part of my job description, I created a perception that those tasks were included in my duties. It was the work equivalent of "common-law marriage." For all intents and purposes, those tasks soon became part of my job because no one could remember a time when I did not do them. Unfortunately, when I felt inevitably overloaded and drew back from those tasks, the action was misconstrued.

I share this to serve as a single warning: even if you are efficient with your time and talents, being unable to say "no" can wreak havoc on the expected ministry work to which you've been called. Creating healthy habits regarding priorities and boundaries early in your ministry will cultivate the ability to discern when to say "no."

Biblical Warning

Matthew 5:33–37 speaks to being people of our word. This section contains the well-known verse that calls for one's "yes to be yes, and no to be no." If you plan to say "yes" to extra tasks, make sure you commit to them with the same passion that you would to your youth ministry. Let your yes be yes, and your no be no. Begin early by instilling a mentality of commitment, boundaries, and follow-through.

CHAPTER 8

Demonstrate Worthwhile Compensation

"It isn't what you have or who you are or where you are or what you are doing that makes you happy or unhappy. It is what you think about it."
- Dale Carnegie -

Being an employee that deserves worthwhile compensation is what everyone desires, and this includes one's employer. With that in mind, it is important to cover some "dos and don'ts" regarding compensation:

Request a detailed job description.
Having a detailed job description empowers you to do what you are paid to do. Without one, a host of duties can be cast upon you and become expected as one of your roles. With a good job description, you will draw a line between what you are paid to do and what you are not.

Know what it costs to live in your community.
Many compare local schoolteachers' salaries with extracurricular responsibilities (coaching, ACT/SAT prep courses, etc.) to

gauge what a local youth ministry job should pay. It is critical to note that these salary packages include retirement and health insurance. Make sure those numbers factor into your analysis.

Do not openly bemoan your compensation.

In many cases, there is a genuine truth that a full-time youth director makes well above the average income of many of their church members. Grumbling to those members will not garner much sympathy.

Instead, DO discuss your financial situation with those in leadership who are in a position to help. If your family is growing or you come to a time of need for various reasons, you should let those in leadership know.

Do not be reckless with church funds.

If you are perceived as reckless with youth ministry funds, the leadership will likely believe fiscal irresponsibility also factors in your personal finances.

Instead, DO demonstrate your appreciation that the church budget comes from the generosity of its members' giving. Ultimately, the church desires for its staff to recognize how blessed they are to receive fair compensation to do what we love. As the conviction to tithe steadily declines in upcoming generations, the attention to wasteful spending increases. Your church will notice your gratitude for their hard-earned tithes through your faithful stewardship of church funds.

Be understanding of the financial situation of your church.

It may well be the case that your church is exceedingly stable financially. However, the general trend in American churches shows tithing to be on the decline. We serve amongst a generation that views the value of tithing as less urgent than the generation before it. Demanding a raise when your church is struggling may be unwise.

Instead, DO approach your leadership with understanding. Speak to your leadership in a way that acknowledges the church's financial situation while clearly articulating your position. They may then be able to offer an agreeable timeline for the church to increase your compensation.

Be cautious adding to your job description merely to receive a well-deserved raise.

Though this has been mentioned in the previous chapter, I felt it important to address this concern more directly. I understand that sometimes taking on more work is the only path forward, but make sure you have given it hard thought and prayer before adding to your duties. Youth ministers should be paid for what they are worth, not necessarily for how much they can juggle at one time.

Instead, DO look into a side job that is not attached to your church work. The term for this is *tent-making* or, more casually, *side hustle.* Many avenues exist that would increase your income and pair well with your ministry. I recommend acquiring the approval of your church. You do not want them to feel as if they have been deprioritized.

Earn a raise before you request one.

This may seem like an obvious point, but you would be surprised at the number of youth directors who feel entitled to a substantial raise after their first-year "commitment" to the church. The reality is, if you have garnered enough fruit to justify a large raise within your first year, they will likely recognize that. Therefore, continue to be a diligent, graceful, content, and peaceful employee. Once you have earned it, request the raise.

Do not request a raise in the beginning or middle of the fiscal year.

Work within the fiscal cycle of your church. Church budgets are carefully and delicately prepared. When requesting a raise, do so as the church is planning the budget for the upcoming fiscal year, so that they are able to adequately prepare.

Be grateful for the raises when you receive them.

If your attitude is one of finally receiving what you deserve, you will likely not endear yourself to church leadership. Endeavor to be noticeably appreciative of your church for making the increased financial commitment to you and your family.

Financial conversations are often difficult and uncomfortable. There can be irreparable damage done to the staff–church relationship due to poor handling of such a delicate and personal issue. Use wisdom, caution, and charity in these discussions.

Biblical Warning

Regarding financial compensation for ministers, Acts 6:2 says, "And the twelve summoned the full number of the disciples and said, 'It is not right that we should give up preaching the word of God to serve tables.'" There is a clear case to be made that ministers of the Word should be free from financial worries so that they can perform the necessary duties to serve the people of their church.

On the other hand, Ecclesiastes 5:10 says, "He who loves money will not be satisfied with money, nor he who loves wealth with his income; this also is vanity." The ministers of the church are not to live with selfish hearts. Thus, there is an expectation on the part of the church, and there is an expectation on the part of the minister. In every aspect of your life, but especially in your first year of ministry, it is important to practice the disciplines of contentment and thanksgiving for all the church gives you.

CHAPTER 9

Prioritize Spiritual Maturity

*"Nobody ever outgrows Scripture; the book widens
and deepens with our years."*
- Charles Spurgeon -

The day we believe that we have uncovered all there is to learn from any portion of Scripture is the day that our spiritual growth begins to stall. The Scriptures are a vast wealth of knowledge about our God and Savior and a never-ending well from which we should drink daily. One cannot mature in his spiritual walk without faithful investment in God's Word.

One of the most powerful tools at the disposal of the devil is that of *pious distraction*. This is when we prioritize good, godly, pious deeds or activities over our relationship with God. In other words, we elevate good things above our spiritual walk. This tends to occur because the things that distract us are indeed good, but when they take precedent over our spiritual health, we have placed them above our relationship with God, causing them to become idols. The label of "workaholic" is not just a secular term. The work of ministry can easily become an idol if we refuse to nourish our spirit. Below are some pitfalls of which to be aware:

Time spent in preparation for teaching is not the same as time spent studying for personal growth

It is easy to blend the two. Both look the same, feel the same, and lead to intellectual knowledge of God and His Word. However, the attitude and context of the approaches are a contrast. Do not make the mistake of confusing ministerial "prepwork" on behalf of teenagers for the personal spiritual nourishment necessary for your own maturation.

Substituting spiritual nourishment with emotional youth ministry moments

In my experience, when students turn to Christ, it is not often in the confines of their bedroom. Rather, it is at summer camp, retreats, or conferences. It is in the moments when they can disconnect from the noise of the world and turn their attention to Christ. Because of this, the conversion experience is often framed around highly emotional experiences. Although I would be wary for this to be your only pattern for conversions, it is the reality of how youth ministry tends to operate. This pattern can be emotionally draining on youth ministers, causing the routine of daily nourishment to seem stale in comparison.

The seminary effect

When questioned about the most challenging aspect of seminary, many pastors will answer, "maintaining consistent spiritual growth and nourishment." For some, seminary was a spiritual desert. On the surface, that seems unlikely since the Word and other ministers constantly surrounded them. In reality, this response gives valuable insight into the heart of man. It is easy to relegate the Word to simple head knowledge. It should serve as a warning to us as to how familiarity can seed personal neglect.

Lack of accountability

Who within your circle of friends is concerned with your spiritual growth? For many of us, we are recognized as spiritual leaders by the church, and as such, we are expected to be deeply committed to our own spiritual nourishment. Often, that is the case. But everyone has droughts, and everyone needs accountability. If you do not have someone holding you accountable in your spiritual walk, I encourage you to make finding that person a priority.

Being a hypocrite

Charging your students to spend consistent devotional time in the Word while you neglect the same is hypocritical at best. I do not believe you can speak with moral authority into teenagers' lives when you are not living to the same standard. Always remember: teenagers have a sharp eye for hypocrisy.

Ignoring your secret sins

Secret sins have a way of haunting ministers. They harden hearts and refuse the discipline of the Gospel. Secret sins almost always become public, resulting in shame that has long-lasting, if not permanent, ramifications for the minister.

Indulging in pornography.

Sadly, internet pornography consumption is rampant in our culture and our churches, partly due to the extraordinary ease of access. Not only is pornography easily accessible, but it's easily concealable. If you are a minister in God's church, internet pornography consumption absolutely cannot be a part of your life. I encourage everyone to have accountability in this area. See the appendix for a list of recommended resources and tools to combat this deadly spiritual epidemic.

Refusing to Sabbath.

God established the Sabbath at the creation of the universe for two purposes: God's glory and the benefit of humankind. When the Lord laid out the day of rest, it was so that man would cease from his labors and abide in the physical and spiritual rest of his God. Since most youth directors work on Sundays, obtaining another day to Sabbath is crucial. I believe that ministry burnout is often the result of a refusal to take a day each week to rest.

Wisdom from the Past

If we ignore the voices of the past, then we will continue to commit the same mistakes. Below are some shared wisdom from godly men before us:

> "It is best to have at least one hour alone with God before engaging in anything else. At the same time, I must be careful not to reckon communion with God by minutes or hours, or by solitude."
> —Robert Murray M'Cheyne

> "Take heed to thyself. Your own soul is your first and greatest care. You know a sound body alone can work with power, much more a healthy soul. Keep a clear conscience through the blood of the Lamb. Keep up close communion with God. Study likeness to Him in all things. Read the Bible for your own growth first, then for your people."
> —Horatius Bonar

"Satan will always find you something to do," he would say, "when you ought to be occupied about that, if it is only arranging a window blind."
—Hudson Taylor

Formulate a Plan

The world will always attempt to disrupt our relationship with God. A harmful error is to present it a chance. I recommend finding a routine and plan that organize your day around devotional time in the Word. Here are some suggestions to make your plan a reality:

Have a Bible reading plan.
There is an abundance of plans and strategies to help you read through the Bible in a year. Find one you like and cling to it. If you miss more than a few days, pick up on the current date and move forward. This approach's notable danger is that one can see the reading plan as a task to be accomplished, not as something to nourish. Slow down and use the reading plan to nourish your soul.

Use devotional guides.
Obtaining a quality devotional guide is incredibly effective for our spiritual nourishment. A devotional guide provides a focus for our prayers, meditations, and application of the Bible. Sometimes we can read a portion of Scripture and miss how it applies to our life. A good devotional plan will walk you through Scripture and help you see the immediate application, as well as the historical implications. This approach's danger is that the focus can shift from the text to the commentary; therefore, do be mindful of that. Charles Spurgeon once said, "Visit many good books, but live in the Bible."

Join a Bible reading group.
Find a group who will work through the Bible with you as an accountability measure. A group such as this will also offer encouragement, community, and perspectives that you might miss otherwise. This approach's danger is that you can substitute the reading group for private devotion if not careful.

Set aside a committed, structured time for personal devotion.
Good habits do not occur by chance. No one accidentally joins a gym and works out. We are wired to be enemies of God, and our hearts are constantly at war with the flesh. We battle the flesh in this area by being disciplined with our time. Be intentional in your personal devotion.

Biblical Warning

I have always regarded the life of Judas Iscariot as fascinating. How could someone who walked with Jesus, ate with him, watched him perform countless miracles, and witness his compassion towards the weak betray the Messiah? How could he hand over someone who probably treated him with higher respect than anyone else before? How does someone who so intimately knew Jesus betray him?

For Judas, it may have been a slow and steady hardening of his heart. Perhaps he followed Jesus out of mere interest and fascination, or possibly because he saw an opportunity to capitalize off the rabbi. Whatever the reason, one thing is certain: proximity doesn't dictate the relationship. One can work in the church and minister to the flock yet have no genuine relationship with Christ. I once heard it said that the power of the Word is such that it cannot be idle: It either hardens hearts or softens hearts; there is nothing in between. Spend time in the Word in a way that softens your hearts. Early in your ministry commit to a life of personal spiritual growth.

CHAPTER 10

Equip Parents

"Hear, O Israel: The Lord our God, the Lord is one. You shall love the Lord your God with all your heart and with all your soul and with all your might. And these words that I command you today shall be on your heart. You shall teach them diligently to your children, and shall talk of them when you sit in your house, and when you walk by the way, and when you lie down, and when you rise. You shall bind them as a sign on your hand, and they shall be as frontlets between your eyes. You shall write them on the doorposts of your house and on your gates."
Deuteronomy 6:4–9

The parenting culture will differ depending on the church which you are privileged to serve. On the one hand, some churches have very engaged parents who are intentionally cultivating discipleship culture on behalf of their children. On the other hand, some churches feel like they hired you to do every bit of that. What do you do in a situation where parents seem to have a minimal drive to disciple their children? As we know, Deuteronomy 6:4–9 makes a clear command: Parents disciple your children. The church's role is to come alongside parents and encourage them as the primary discipleship agents in their children's lives. There are many books and resources that give in-depth training on this issue. However, I want to point out a few "dos and don'ts:"

Get to know the parents of your students.
Before you can influence your students' parents', you need to be their friend. This does not mean that you will be inviting each other to movie nights and double dates, although that is not a terrible idea! This means that you and the parents share a real relationship, one that instills trust and honesty.

Don't beat them up.
Usually, parents are striving to do their very best. No parent hopes to fail. Most desire to be better at this divine calling and are painfully aware of the areas where they fall short. Discipling teenagers is a complicated task. Parents do not need you to lay guilt and shame upon them, especially if you do not have teenagers of your own.

Be informed.
This points back to the chapter on teachability. You are hired to be the resident expert on teenagers in your church, so be the expert. If a parent comes to you with a new teen trend or some viral challenge, you do not want that conversation to be the first you are hearing about these things. Find ways to be aware of culture without being influenced by it.

Enlist them as volunteers.
The rule of thumb is that a small group leader needs to be "not a parent, not a peer." However, engaging your parents in other roles is critical for their investment in you and the youth ministry. Involve parents in your ministry in any way that you are

able. This will provide them some ownership of the ministry and some respect for how you influence their children.

Point them to experts.
Sometimes, the best approach is to have the right parenting resources available to them. Make sure your parents know what experts your church trusts and how they can access those resources.

"Neighborhood Students"

I do not know how you choose to identify the students whose parents do not attend your church. I call them "neighborhood students." These are the students that I have no real parental contact or knowledge of their parents' church background. It is with these students that you must be particularly intentional in discipling. It is possible that they are not receiving much, if any, spiritual guidance at home. Invest heavily in these students.

The Payoff Is This

First, you are helping to fulfill the commands of Deuteronomy 6:6–7. Second, by encouraging and equipping your church's parents to disciple their children, it will help free up your time to invest more in the students who are not receiving the same spiritual leadership at home.

Biblical Warning

The Bible makes it clear: the parents are to be the main discipleship agents for their children. The role of the church is to come alongside and help. Deuteronomy 6:6–7 says, "And these words that I command you today shall be on your heart. You shall teach them diligently to your children, and shall talk of them when you sit in your house, and when you walk by the way, and when you lie down, and when you rise." Be careful not to fall into the trap of believing that you are the "parent whisperer" and you are there to be a specialized tutor because parents have not figured out how to disciple their children. Lean on the parents, allow them to lean on you, and facilitate ways to assist each other.

PART 2

Understanding Vision and Strategy

For fruitful ministry to exist, the leader must draw a clear distinction between vision and strategy. The church of Jesus Christ is committed to proclaim to all creation the great "why" of man's existence. What is the purpose for which humankind was formed? As the *Westminster Confession of Faith* rightly summarizes, it is to "glorify God and enjoy him forever." Accordingly, we are exhorted in Matthew 28:18–20: "And Jesus came and said to them, 'All authority in heaven and on earth has been given to me. Go therefore and make disciples of all nations, baptizing them in the name of the Father and of the Son and of the Holy Spirit, teaching them to observe all that I have commanded you. And behold, I am with you always, to the end of the age.'"

Our teaching (doctrine) is the Gospel of Jesus Christ, the Son of God (Mark 1:1). The Gospel is the "whole purpose of God" (Acts 20:27). Thus, doctrine is the "what" of the church's mission, found in the Bible alone, the inerrant and infallible Word of God.

I desire to take our great mission and the truth that undergirds it and approach it specifically from the vantage point of the first year of youth ministry. To do this, I believe that a youth ministry's "where" and "how" need to be clear and practical. In other words, there needs to be a clear understanding of vision and strategy and how they differ and complement one another.

Vision

Vision is defined as "the overarching direction for the ministry, as given to us from God's Word and applied to youth ministry." In other words, *vision* is the "where" of ministry, answering the crucial question of "where is this ministry headed?" All ministry vision must flow out of the mission and teaching of the Gospel.

Thus, the overarching direction for the ministry must be given to us from God's Word. If the Word of Christ is not the standard for a church's ministry vision, then the church is nothing more than another earthly institution founded on worldly principles. Biblical mission and scriptural doctrine will result in Gospel vision.

Strategy

We will define *strategy* as "the steps one takes to implement and make the vision a reality." Often referred to as the "how" of the great mission, the strategy fills in the numerous and varied "nuts and bolts" of "getting the job done."

CHAPTER 11

Establishing Vision

"Where there is no vision, there is no hope."
- George Washington Carver -

In every ministry, within its vision, there should be the desire to make disciples, baptize new converts, and teach the commands of God. There should be the "destination" of being conformed to the image of Jesus (Romans 8:29; 1 John 3:2). The "where" of vision focuses on Christ in sanctification as much as Christ in conversion. These are destinations of a sort that we should want to see every disciple realize (Colossians 1:28). With that in mind, it is imperative to make sure that your ministry vision is both broad and deep in its direction taken from the Scriptures. A ministry vision needs to be an all-encompassing approach to Christian discipleship.

It is necessary to be aware of some common pitfalls of casting a vision:

Ministry vision should not be abstract.
The "end game" of youth ministry should be as concrete as the truth of the Bible. The apostle Paul knew precisely where he wanted to go, proclaiming Christ that he "might present every man complete in Christ" (Colossians 1:24). The foundation of a

ministry's vision either enables it to stand or causes it to fall. If the guiding principle of a ministry vision is man-made, then it will ultimately fail. However, if God's Word confirms it, then it will endure.

Ministry vision should be harmonious with the goals of the church.

Even as your vision needs to be tangible, so does your understanding of your congregation's expectations. You may have an idea for a particular direction, but that does not mean that the rest of your church does. Where do you want your students to be spiritually when they graduate from high school? Is it the same place envisioned by their parents and church leadership?

Ministry vision is not your programs.

This is where many confuse strategy with vision. The "how" needs to follow a well-thought-out and well-articulated "where." Once your destination's clarity becomes subordinate to activities, you become rudderless; you are now drifting without any central direction. Do the work of establishing the "where" before introducing the "how."

That leaves the question: How do we begin to establish a vision? I believe there are two ways to do this. First, don't become too specific too soon. Second, don't remain too vague for too long.

Mistake 1: Too Specific Too Soon

New or prospective youth directors often feel pressured into setting forth agendas with church leadership before they know enough about the congregation. This error is usually made "on the fly." In other words, you are in an interview or meeting, and you share a detailed vision for the church before you have substantial knowledge or investment. You may not know that the church participates in foreign missions. You probably have no idea why outreach to the local schools has not been effective in the past. In other words, you have yet to grasp the full range of past failure and success that should be appreciated before you can begin to move the church forward. Be warned: once you commit to a plan, you may be held to it!

The downside to committing yourself to a vision before you are ready is that you run the risk of appearing to fail when, in reality, you committed to an uninformed vision. A likely consequence is that you may appear to be someone who could not make their vision a reality. People may then begin to criticize your strategy, which will be treated in the next chapter.

Everyone should have an answer to "What is your vision for this group?" But in your first year, the answer needs to be one that abides within the Great Commission instead of assurances to unrealizable ideals. "Promise less, do more" is the idea. Some advice on being patient with the particulars in casting a vision with your church leadership:

Do not change ANYTHING in your first month.
Restraint in this area is tough to manage. Many youth directors arrive and instantly want to make significant changes. They hope to correct what is "wrong," eliminate what is broken, and add their own personality and "flavor" to the ministry. But, what would happen if you committed the first month to watching and analyzing what works and what does not? What if you spent a month assessing your volunteers and building rapport with students instead of directing your creative energies on new programs? Be a student of your new church. Take some time before making significant changes. You really do have time! Besides, infusing your personality and energy into the room will be a massive change for the students in and of itself.

Find out what the students and the parents want and need.
You will often find that the parents and students want the same things, but they articulate those desires differently. Take some time in your first months to meet one-on-one with parents, host a parent "town hall" (do not insult the last person), and have a system for gathering information from your parents and students about the changes they would like to see or the elements that they wholeheartedly support.

God calls parents to be the primary spiritual guides for their children, but you are hired to be the spiritual leader and vision caster of that group. If the parents' desires are not in line with your own, then my advice would be to have an intentional conversation with the church leadership about how to proceed. As always, in navigating the manifold and various pitfalls of youth ministry, you want to tread lightly here, soliciting the wisdom and support of your senior pastor and other church leaders.

Go on the trips your students love.
Spend your first year attending the camps and events to which your students are attached. Even though your experience and comfort level lies in another direction, do not be fast to impose your favorites on the group. Once you have earned their confidence, then you can execute any wanted changes. Many accidentally sow bad seeds with an ill-timed move that upends cherished tradition.

Learn where your students are spiritually.
It isn't easy to set reasonable goals for your students' spiritual walk if you do not know how far they need to go in the time they have left to be in the group. Are your students still on spiritual milk, or are they ready for something more? Unfortunately, attaining this knowledge will take time. Your new students may like you, but they may not necessarily trust you yet, and neither do the parents. Finding honest vulnerability among the teenagers

with whom you are ministering demands relationship and genuine care. Accomplishing this must be a priority in your first year so that you can begin to assess the biblical and spiritual maturity of your new group. Identifying the spiritual maturity of your students is critical in determining a ministry vision. The reason is simple: asking too much can discourage them and expecting too little fails to be faithful to your calling.

Thus, the most significant danger of making "Mistake 1: Being Too Specific Too Soon" is that you make important and long-term decisions without earning the trust of the students, parents, and church that you are seeking to lead. Be patient in your first year.

Mistake 2: Too Vague for Too Long

If committing to an inflexible vision too early resides on one end of the spectrum, then remaining too vague for too long is at the other end. Remaining too vague or uncommitted to a vision leaves a ministry without direction. Sadly, this at times is the state of many youth ministries. It seems as if everyone is just there, having fun and trying to do the best they can. As an illustration, imagine that a landowner invited ten people to build a large barn. All of the supplies were provided, and a qualified, licensed contractor was on-site to supervise the project. But the only instructions were, "Build the structure." The workers and their contractor would have no concept of what they were building, even though everything was provided.

If they could guess correctly and build a barn, the barn would surely not be built according to the landowner's needs. The doors may be too small, the horses may not have adequate stalls, and the hayloft may have been overlooked. Without a clear goal in mind, everyone could work their hardest and still not achieve their goal.

Here are some tips for directing vision:

See what the other ministries in your church are trying to accomplish.
Is there a common vision in which the youth ministry could partner with the rest of the church? Are there particular elements that can only be properly fulfilled by the youth ministry?

Is the vision for your group feasible financially and geographically?
For example, a rural church will probably have a difficult time sustaining a thriving inner-city ministry. A church that is limited in its finances will struggle to create a five-year partnership with a mission organization in Africa. Every church is not called to do everything equally. However, every church is called to be as effective as it can be for the Gospel in the circumstances God has set it.

What cultural hurdles will you have to overcome to get everyone on board?
Sometimes this can be challenging, which is why I counsel patience in an overly detailed vision of your first year. However, if you wait too long, you lose your "fresh eyes" and the unbiased perspective on your church. Recognize the obstacles within your first year, or you may find out that you have become the obstruction.

Handling Critics

Every church has those who have a lot to say! Sadly, we are all wired to "gawk and squawk" when things go awry due to our sinful natures. You will have critics in your ministry. Some of them may even be people you believed to be on your team. They will find any little problem, your responsibility or not, and take note. Over time, this will begin to form a narrative in people's perceptions of you. The more mistakes you make, the louder the critics can become to the ears of the church. When there is no set direction in a ministry, every determination then lacks the vision's authority and is open to legitimate complaints. A good vision informs and defends what a ministry does.

It is essential before you set your vision to ensure that it is fully vetted by your pastor, youth committee, and church leadership. This grants you the benefit of the all-powerful "we." No longer do you say, "I decided," but you say, "We felt...." This shifts the authority from you alone to that of the leadership. Securing the support of your committee and church leadership protects and credits your vision.

Establishing a healthy vision is vital for a fruitful ministry. But we must be conscious of the dangers of committing too early or waiting too long. The church is looking to you for wisdom in leadership, clarity in goals, and trusting you to take steps to make that vision a reality. This is where strategy comes into play.

Why Are YOU in the Student Ministry?

I have worked with student leaders over the years who practically "fell into" student ministry. Youth directors made enormous impressions on their lives while they were teenagers, and they remember that. They love working with students, and they love Jesus! All of these things are good and are needed in the church. However, there is a big difference between those things and a ministry calling. If you are grappling to establish a vision for your church, it could be because you are wrestling with your "calling."

Key Questions to Ask Leadership

When considering your ministry vision, be sure to ask your church leadership two specific questions:

1. How can I align the student ministry vision with the church's?

This is supremely important. If the student ministry vision does not align with the church's, it will become a "siloed" ministry and would lack the full support of both the congregation and church leadership.

2. How will I know when I am successful at my job?

Knowing the answer to this question will guard against two common ministry emotions: feelings of underappreciation and lack of confidence in ministry vision. Ministry is dissimilar from many other occupations because there are seldom clear progress markers. As a result, churches often determine "success" according to an internal rubric that requires that you search out the answer to this question. Unfortunately, there are all too many churches and youth directors who fail to communicate the answer to this question, and the result is often a brief relationship.

Biblical Warning

Vision is an important theme in the Bible. When contemplating what it means to sow seeds that lead to a fruitful ministry vision, I am reminded of the parable of the talents found in Matthew 25:14–30.

In this parable, the master left town and entrusted his servants with modest amounts of money. Two of the servants, knowing their master well, invested and multiplied the funds. Upon their master's return, these two servants were honored and trusted with much more.

Rather than risk losing his investment, the third servant buried the talents in the ground. When the master returned, the servant gave back the original sum of money to his master. When asked why he did not invest like the others, the third servant replied, "Because I was afraid."

The servants had a responsibility. They knew their master well, and each knew what their master would demand of them. But only certain ones were faithful in what was entrusted to them.

Like the men in the parable, we are called to be faithful in what our master has given us. In other words, we are to invest what we are given in a way that multiplies. Our talents, skills, and circumstances are allotted to us so that we might glorify God and advance His Kingdom.

Do not allow fear of failure to prevent you from leading your ministry in a manner that increases and edifies the Kingdom of God!

CHAPTER 12

Mapping-Out Strategy

"People in any organization are always attached to the obsolete—the things that should have worked but did not, the things that once were productive and no longer are."

- Peter Drucker -

W ith the ministry's vision explained, the development of a strategy should follow. Be advised: One of the most harmful oversights that any ministry leader can make is introducing a strategy before establishing a ministry vision. The vision is the overarching goal, and the strategy is the process taken to achieve that goal.

Let's return to the barn illustration. If you were directed to build a barn and supplied with all of the necessary provisions, the barn would be your vision. The instructions and steps you take to complete the barn would be your strategy. You would employ various tools for different jobs, concentrate on some areas more than others, and hire workers to complete tasks you would be unable to accomplish alone. This is what your strategy should look like. It is the "how" in the execution of your ministry.

Developing a Ministry Strategy

Developing a ministry strategy will likely be one of the most challenging aspects of youth ministry. A proper strategy answers the question, "How are you going to execute to realize your vision?" Many use a different word for strategy: *Planning*. A well-crafted plan systematizes all the various activities, ministry elements, and interactions built into your ministry. That being said, how does one go about forming their ministry strategy?

Pray

Although this may seem like an obvious first step, it isn't always treated as such. Strategy tends to fall into the realm of our intellect. It is where a youth director can be creative, organized, and intentional in their ministry. Thus, it can often be seen as a task to be executed rather than a spiritual goal to be accomplished. We must remember that we are simply laborers in the field, hoping to reap the harvest that God has in store. Cover your ministry strategy in prayer, inviting your church and leadership to do the same.

Collect Information

You will not be able to plan an effective ministry strategy without truly knowing your church. Proper planning for useful activities and ministry programs require a certain amount of reconnaissance work, or else there may be frustration. For example: If you are unaware of how many students typically attend Sunday night youth, how many hotdogs do you purchase for an event? You would have collected this information before beginning your cookout. Details like this are examples of the information collection required to implement your strategy. Listed below are some principles that I believe are critical to developing a ministry strategy:

Consider your students.
How many students attend Sunday morning worship, and how many attend youth activities? Ministry Architects suggests that the standard for healthy youth group attendance is 10%–15% of a church's overall Sunday participation.[6] Additionally, remember to account for any students whose parents do not attend your church.

Consider your budget.
What is the youth ministry budget? One can learn plenty about the value assigned to a church's youth ministry by studying the budget set aside to support it. Are you financially capable of planning large events? Within your budget, have you accounted for the means to feed the students each week?

Consider your community.
One of your strategy's foci should be to cultivate the students' loyalty so that you can regularly invest in the lives of the church's teenagers. Are there other community activities pulling students away during your regularly scheduled youth nights? Do you need to adjust times or switch days?

Consider your students' interests.
Much of your strategy will be based upon both the personal and collective interests of your students. If you minister to students who thrive in athletic competition, then maybe a Mario Kart tournament is not the most productive use of your time. You

---

6. Safstrom, A. (2019, March 05). "Youth Ministry Norms." Retrieved December 22, 2020, from https://ministryarchitects.com/youth-ministry-norms/

need to know your students' interests to develop a strategy with which they will connect.

Consider your students spiritual standing.
Some of you will be called to churches in which the majority of the students are not focused on their spiritual relationship with God. This means that your strategy may initially be one that offers more milk than solid food (Hebrews 5:12; 1 Corinthians 3:2). Others of you will serve at churches that will likely generate the future leaders of the church. Knowing the flock to which you minister is vital.

Consider your cultural context.
Is your church in a rural or urban context? I have a friend who serves at a church in rural Mississippi. For outreach events, they host dove hunts and mud-riding nights— and it WORKS. If I were to try this in Jackson, it would not produce nearly the same participation level. Being able to put your finger on the pulse of your community will pay instant dividends.

Study the Data

Once you have taken the time to accumulate all of this helpful information, you will be ready to evaluate the data. I would advise some trial-and-error activities to see if you are properly interpreting the collected data on your church and students before finalizing your ministry strategy. Discuss the information with your parents and church leadership. Meet with other established youth directors in the community and ask for their input regarding your work. Make sure you get this right!

Prioritize

Now that you have assessed all of that information, it is time to outline your ministry's priorities. Here are some points of consideration:

Prioritize from the inside out.
You were hired first and foremost to minister to the students in your church, not those outside of it. Begin internally, then expand (think concentric circles).

Find a balance.
You want to ensure that your strategy strikes a healthy balance of spiritual nourishment, evangelistic outreach, and fellowship activities. Strive to be the group that does life together as well as worships together.

Make sure your strategy harmonizes with your vision.
Remember, vision informs strategy, not the other way around. Your strategy must carry the students toward the goal expressed in your vision. If you find that you have a program element that does not fit, you may need to reevaluate its effectiveness within your strategy.

Execution

There are numerous ministry strategies. Your strategy may look different from those of the churches nearby. This is because every church has particular areas that need attention. However, I believe that some foundational strategy elements must be in place: Scripture, Prayer, Worship, Missions, Discipleship, Apologetics, and Outreach. From there, secondary elements such as:

style, regularity, group size, environment, and timing are all dependent on your ministry context, and these will differ from church to church.

Keep in mind, it is always better to develop an achievable strategy than a massively comprehensive but unattainable one. In other words, don't build a barn for which you cannot afford to keep the hay stocked. Below are some extra tips for developing your ministry strategy:

Start small and expand as you are able.
Make sure the "meat and potatoes" are covered before deciding to add the side dishes. All Scripture is equally true, but all Scripture is not equally important. The story of the floating ax-head in 2 Kings 6 is equally true as the death and resurrection of Jesus. However, knowing this story is not equally important as knowing about Christ's death and resurrection. The same goes for student ministry strategy. Be sure to prioritize essential ministry elements.

Be sure that your strategy supports your church's vision.
You will find it much easier to gather support and volunteers if they are familiar with the strategy which you are implementing. One way to do this is by mirroring the church's ministry strategy by partnering in local missions and participating in intergenerational activities.

Engage volunteers.
You should aim to strengthen weaknesses and improve strengths with the volunteers surrounding your ministry. Engage and encourage them without ceasing.

Collect input from your leadership.
Launching a comprehensive ministry strategy is best done when the entire leadership is excited and energized by what you are

preparing. Listen to their counsel and use wisdom in implementing their input.

Pray.
We are to do all things to the glory of God. Our ministries should reflect the will of God for our church. Spend time with the Lord, praying for guidance and wisdom as you structure a ministry that fulfills the Great Commission and glorifies God.

Map It Out.
Many often skip this step. It is imperative to put your strategy and schedule down on paper to ensure you are neither overwhelming or underwhelming your church. The families in your church are busy. By mapping it out, you will be in a position to plan accordingly.

Implement.
Once you have everything in place, it is time to set a strategy "start date" and begin implementing your new plan. It WILL need to be tweaked and modified as you go, but I would maintain that a strategy that is incapable of adjusting is one that is unable to go the distance. A word to the wise: do not allow pride to hinder you from fine-tuning your strategy!

Communicate.
Distribute your new calendar and make sure everyone knows about any changes. Host a parents' meeting so that you can clearly communicate the "what" and "why" behind that which has been scheduled.

Reevaluate annually.
Carey Nieuwhof is a well-known church visionary and strategist. He has authored numerous books and is a prominent church conference speaker. As culture has changed, he has recreated

and adjusted his approach to church ministry to adapt. Regarding strategy, he says, "Just because you've found something that works doesn't mean you've found what works best. Just because you've made progress doesn't mean you've met your potential." In other words, just because your strategy works does not mean you are finished striving to improve it. In your first year at a new church, it is crucial to sow seeds of intentional strategy that will be fruitful in the years to come.

Biblical Warning

When you consider strategies and programs that need to be implemented, beware of an overly casual approach in your Christian leadership. We can often hold our youth ministry in the shallow end by structuring the ministry so that it doesn't challenge the students. I try to remember how Paul reminds the Corinthian church, "I fed you with milk, not solid food, for you were not ready for it" (1 Corinthians 3:2). In other words, Paul recognized that his flock should be growing and cultivating a deeper knowledge of God, but instead, they still needed to be fed like children. Never be satisfied with feeding our church like children, but instead nurture them towards a deeper knowledge and understanding of our great God.